THE HARRY P

By the same author

Hagbane's Doom
Gublak's Greed
Surin's Revenge
Tergan's Lair
Feldrog's String
A Closer Look at His Dark Materials
Out Here
Issues Facing Society
Handling Your Money
Fear Not
The Healthy Alternative
A Touch of Love
A Distant Shore
Parenting Teenagers

The Harry Potter Effect

Taking a closer look at the complete series

JOHN HOUGHTON

David C Cook
transforming lives together

THE HARRY POTTER EFFECT
Published by David C. Cook
Kingsway Communications Ltd
Lottbridge Drove, Eastbourne BN23 6NT, England

David C. Cook
4050 Lee Vance View, Colorado Springs, CO 80918 U.S.A.

David C. Cook Distribution Canada
55 Woodslee Avenue, Paris, Ontario, Canada N3L 3E5

David C. Cook and the graphic circle C logo
are registered trademarks of Cook Communications Ministries.

All rights reserved. No part of this publication may be reproduced or transmitted in any form or by any means, electronic or mechanical, including photocopy, recording, or any information storage and retrieval system, without permission in writing from the publisher.

The publishers will permit up to 400 words of prose to be extracted for non-commercial purposes or for review, subject to full acknowledgement being given to author, title of work, publisher's name and date of publication.

The Web site addresses recommended throughout this book are offered as a resource to you. These Web sites are not intended in any way to be or imply an endorsement on the part of David C. Cook, nor do we vouch for their content.

Unless otherwise shown, biblical quotations are from the Holy Bible:
New International Version, © 1973, 1978, 1984
by the International Bible Society.
NKJV = New King James Version

ISBN 978 1 842913 62 8

© 2007 John Houghton
The right of John Houghton to be identified as author of this work has been asserted by him in accordance with the Copyright, Designs and Patents Act 1988.

Cover design by Pinnacle Creative UK
Cover images © Bridgetjones, Webking, Marchodnett,
Aliencat, Stajduhar, Luminis I Dreamstime.com

Printed in Great Britain
First Edition 2007

1 2 3 4 5 6 7 8 9 10

060607

Contents

Preface   7
Introduction   10

1. At Face Value   15
2. Just Imagine   23
3. The World Between Worlds   36
4. The Mythic Journey   47
5. Talking of Witches   61
6. Worlds Apart   77
7. Deathly Horrors   89
8. The Politics of Power   98
9. A Better Story   105
10. Train Up a Child   113

Appendix   125

To Debbie, Matthew and Sharon,
Steve and Emma
who by love and prayer are training six to be wise.

'Those who are wise will shine
like the brightness of the heavens, and those
who lead many to righteousness, like the
stars for ever and ever.'
(Daniel 12:3)

Preface

With the publication of *Harry Potter and the Deathly Hallows* we had the long awaited *dénouement* and the resolution of the mystery that J K Rowling had teased us with for the previous ten years. Finally we knew the whole story and all the important questions were answered.

The author could justly celebrate. Some of her critics had to eat their words. Others now wish to consider the impact of the series on our lives and the lives of our children. What is the Harry Potter effect? To what extent have the books influenced our basic assumptions, our beliefs and our behaviour? How much has it changed the way we think? Why is it the greatest publishing phenomenon of our generation? Sales of the first six books have exceeded 325 million copies and this seventh volume became another record-breaking bestseller on its first day. The first five films have grossed over 4 billion dollars, with similar success to follow. That is to say nothing of the merchandising billions and the Harry Potter theme park being built in Florida. The author herself is reported to have become a billionaire on the basis of her books and has received the OBE.

Translated into many languages, *Harry Potter* is a phenomenon on a global scale and is set to remain so for a long time to come. Part of the reason for that success is that the Harry Potter books are not so much children's books as books about children and teenagers that deal with the predominantly adult themes of love and death. As such, they have accessed the older teens and adult markets just as much as the traditional children's market. Using a classically mythic structure and telling the stories with flair, imagination and wit, Rowling has pressed all the right cultural buttons too. In *Harry Potter* we find not only some rattling good yarns but an exploration of alienation and fear. We observe the contemporary political and social effects of terrorism, state paranoia and media manipulation, along with rising fascism. Rowling's world also appeals to our desire to escape the humdrum impersonality of consumerism and soulless technology. Instead, we are drawn into a nostalgic world of fantasy and romance, a gothic mix of the fantastic and the macabre, driven along by a political power struggle. In this world of colourful magic we find fulfilled our desire for heroes, for courage and hope.

Has J K Rowling done more? Have her books had a spiritual impact? Are our beliefs, our values, modified as a result of reading them? Has she encouraged the growth of witchcraft and the occult, or has she subtly promoted the Christian faith? What impact has she had on our world view? Have the horror and macabre elements of her stories developed, disturbed, or hardened children's emotional development? Has she weaned them away from the cynicism of Playstation-type war games? Do her books restore imagination to a generation dulled by excessively left-brained school examinations? Can we commend the books and films to our children, or should we express caution, or even impose an outright ban? In a world saturated with media entertainment, should we even care?

PREFACE

In my first reflection on the phenomenon, *A Closer Look at Harry Potter* (Kingsway Publications 2001), I commented on the first four Harry Potter books. In this second volume, while covering some similar ground, I have explored the entire Harry Potter series and the subsequent developments in our culture. As before, those who desire an unqualified condemnation or commendation of Rowling's work had better look elsewhere; they will be disappointed. Those who wish to discern between good and evil in our current generation and who want to produce culturally literate, wise, God-respecting children who know how to have fun without regrets and who can make a positive impact on their world, should read on.

John Houghton
August 2007

Introduction

Imagine a baby narrowly escaping death in an assault that killed both his parents. The unfortunate infant is taken in with reluctance by the most appalling and bourgeois aunt and uncle that you could think of. They hate everything about him and conspire never to tell him his true identity. At the age of eleven the child is contacted out of the blue and told that he has a place at an exclusive boarding school somewhere in the north of Britain. Upon his arrival he makes his first real friends in life and together they have lots of fun. In the course of time they uncover a dark plot to steal a priceless jewel hidden in the school buildings. The would-be thief turns out to be none other than the person who had murdered the child's parents and who now wants to complete the job by killing the boy.

Now call the child Harry Potter and make him the gifted offspring of a witch and a wizard, who without his being aware of it is destined for a great future that is yet to be revealed. Introduce a complex society of witches skilled in the magic arts and operating secretively in a fantastical parallel world to our own – so close, however, that your neighbour down the street might easily be a practising member. Fill this plot with plenty of wit, and parody the 'people into frogs and flying broomsticks' notions of witchcraft while, at the same time, running a much darker tale of good magic versus bad magic.

It turns out that Voldemort, the arch villain and murderer of Harry Potter's parents, was so weakened by his attempt to kill the baby that he was reduced to a disembodied shade, for the child had received some special and unexpected power from the death of his mother. However, rumour has it that Voldemort is seeking to re-establish his evil regime and, although most of the witches in this society use magic for good purposes, some who have gone over to the Dark side – the Death Eaters – are helping him fulfil his plans.

Harry Potter is at Hogwarts, a boarding school for young wizards. He travels there, along with other young witches, from platform nine-and-three-quarters at King's Cross, a magic doorway into a romantic and nostalgic world of steam trains, a forbidding lake, a turreted castle of great halls and secret passageways, and a dark and dangerous forest. The jewel is the philosopher's stone and Harry, with the help of his friends and the benevolent head teacher, Albus Dumbledore, faces and defeats the incarnation of Voldemort when he is manifested in a member of staff.

So begins the *Harry Potter* series by J K Rowling – so begins, too, the biggest children's book phenomenon of all time, bringing delight to children, teachers, parents and publishers alike, and making the author a very wealthy and respected writer.

---

[1] Karen Jo Gounaud, 'Should Harry Potter go to public school?', Family Friendly Libraries, October 1999.

[2] *Citizen*, a magazine of the Focus on the Family organisation, 1999.

[3] Lindy Beam, 'Plugged in – What shall we do with Harry?', Focus on the Family, July 2000.

It all sounds like good clean fun, and good luck to the author. Yet while the world mostly applauds, Christians in particular are divided and many have called for the books to be banned from state schools and public libraries. These are, after all, books about witchcraft, and the Scriptures make it clear that involvement with the occult is a serious no-no. Typical of the early responses was Family Friendly Libraries (FFL): 'Harry is a warlock, his dad was a warlock and his mother was a witch,' and later, the 'Harry Potter series focuses on the dark side of religion . . . the power is in self-centred pagan worship and magic, not in the righteous God of the world's great religions'.[1] FFL believed that the books were inappropriate for reading in state schools. Atlanta educator John Andrew Murray observed: 'By disassociating magic and supernatural evil, it becomes possible to portray occult practices as good and healthy. It is the duty of Christian parents to oppose Harry Potter, since the Bible condemns witchcraft (Deuteronomy 18:9–12) and tells Christians to "avoid every kind of evil" (1 Thessalonians 5:22).'[2]

Not all wanted to go that far; taking a more tolerant view of the series, Lindy Beam, Youth Culture Analyst of Focus on the Family stated that 'children who read about Harry will probably discover little to nothing about the true world of the occult'. She quoted Charles Colson when he described Rowling's magic as 'purely mechanical, as opposed to occultic'. Even so, she recognised that witchcraft was 'portrayed positively' and found 'the spiritual fault of Harry Potter' to be not so much that 'it plays to the dark supernatural powers, but that it doesn't acknowledge any supernatural powers or moral authority at all'.[3]

With views like these doing the rounds it's hardly surprising that, in spite of the immense popularity of the books, Christian booksellers refused to stock them. According to reports and interviews at the Christian Booksellers Association convention 2000 held in New Orleans, the reasons given ranged from a policy of stocking only biblically based materials through to a concern that Harry Potter may provide an easy way into witchcraft.

Other Christians are much more positive about Harry Potter, notable among whom is John Granger whose book *Looking for God in Harry Potter*[4] sees the series as a covert Christian allegory arising directly from Rowling's professed Christian faith. We shall comment on this view later on.

The initial furore may have died down, but we now live in a post-Potter world and the fact is, whatever we Christians say or do, our children will be hard put to avoid the *Harry Potter* phenomenon even if they want to. It is now part of our cultural milieu – in our schools, on our library shelves, in our bookshops and on our screens. It can't be ignored. Our aim then, in this book, is to look at some of the key issues raised by the *Harry Potter* books – issues that every Christian parent, grandparent, aunt or uncle, Sunday school teacher, children's or youth worker, schoolteacher and church leader must understand if they are to raise up a Spirit-filled generation of children who love God and who love their neighbours.

---

[4] Tyndale House 2004.

1
At Face Value

> Latin is a dead language
> As dead as dead can be
> Then up rose J K Rowling
> And gave us *Potire!* [1]

We should be grateful to J K Rowling: the *Harry Potter* books, with their mix of values and their wide appeal, provide us with an excellent opportunity to exercise some discernment about the spirit of the age and to examine the relevance of the gospel message in the context of our contemporary culture.

To begin with, it is only right and proper that we should take the author and her stories at their face value. J K Rowling is, without doubt, a gifted writer and one who has produced a series of very readable books that has

---

[1] From the childhood version I learned: Latin is a dead language/As dead as dead can be/It killed the rotten Romans/And now it's killing me! *Potire* – Latin: to put in the power of. If Harry comes from the Sanskrit *Hare*, then Harry Potter might mean, *to put in the power of him who removes illusion*, or *to put in the power of the energy of God*. In Christian language, *the anointed one*, no less! Whether Rowling ever intended this is unknown.

appealed to children, teenagers and adults alike. She speaks of her own quite ordinary background with an engaging modesty. Born in 1965 in Chipping Sodbury in Wiltshire, England, she attended Wyedean Comprehensive School before going on to Exeter University to study French and Classics, where she gained a double first. At the age of 26 she went abroad to teach English as a foreign language in Portugal. She married and had a daughter, Jessica. Then life took a downturn and she found herself divorced and living on state benefit in Edinburgh, yet determined to finish the first *Harry Potter* novel. Her subsequent rise to fame – from rags to witches – is, like Harry Potter himself, now legendary. Yet Rowling remains modest and greets the outstanding success of her work with wry bemusement. Now married to Neil Murray, a medical practitioner, both continue to work, believing this to be a good model for their children, Jessica, David and Mackenzie. She actively campaigns for good causes, in particular for research into multiple sclerosis, the disease that killed her mother. She is also a professing Christian, a member of the Scottish Episcopalian Church, though she is quoted as saying: 'like Graham Greene, my faith is sometimes about if my faith will return. It's important to me.'[2]

The books themselves, aimed initially at the 8 to 14-year-old audience but read by many adults, are well crafted, entertaining, humorous and imaginative, and they make for a good read. Jo Rowling has the rare gift of a fine writer: she stirs the imagination of the reader to picture what she is writing about. Her visual and comic style lets you see the grotesque Dursley family; the *olde worlde* steam train journey to the sombre castle; the moving figures in the portraits on

---

[2] *Tatler* magazine, 10 January, 2006.

the walls; the magical banqueting hall with its ever-changing ceiling; the wacky sky-borne game of Quidditch; the secret wizard street in London, Diagon Alley (diagonally, diagonal ley – one of Rowling's many clever word plays), with its weird and wonderful shops – and plenty more besides.

She also writes something more than adventure stories, for her characters, though often larger than life (literally so with Hagrid), are not the predictable superheroes of Hollywood zapping everyone in sight like intergalactic cowboys and Indians, with a few trite, sentimental clichés thrown in to give some pseudo-value to the action. Harry Potter's world is a sternly moral one, where lines are drawn between good and evil, and where good wins through in the end because of an underlying system of values that says it should. Furthermore, the triumphs are not cheap; there is a price to pay, lessons have to be learned and choices must be made that carry consequences. As an example, when Harry is before the Sorting Hat he feels drawn to the nasty Slytherin House but he asks inside himself not to go there. He is put instead into the noble Gryffindor House. Dumbledore later explains: 'It is our choices, Harry, that show what we truly are, far more than our abilities.'

These choices are sometimes painful and costly for Harry, as when he saves his spiteful cousin, Dudley, from the Dementors only to find himself facing expulsion from Hogwarts as a consequence. A harder choice is when Dumbledore insists on Harry plying him with a poisonous potion that will make it possible for them to obtain a horcrux, even though the potion looks set to kill Dumbledore in the process. Hardest of all is when, at the end, he leaves behind his loved ones and goes to face Voldemort in the Forbidden Forest in the certain knowledge that he will die at the tyrant's hands without resisting.

This gives the tales an edge of realism. Rowling avoids the sentimentality characteristic of much fantasy writing. Harry Potter isn't a picture-perfect hero, and he certainly isn't a metaphor for Jesus! He does tell lies and break the rules at times. His character is being formed as he learns to make right choices, and sometimes he gets it wrong. It is this very humanness that makes him so appealing, and which sets him in stark contrast to his Muggle (non-magic) guardians and those who serve the Dark Powers, both of whom alike lack humanity and virtue. Harry Potter is vulnerable, often indignant about his lot in life and feeling powerless in the face of events beyond his understanding. Many a child can identify with him.

He is also growing up, as are his friends, and although he is becoming more skilled simultaneously with the rising power of Voldemort, he is also facing the realities of being a teenager. This includes feeling misunderstood, being subject to rages and bad language, and taking a romantic interest in girls – though in this form of magic he is hardly an adept. (We welcome Rowling's innocent portrayal of teenage falling in love with its emphasis on discovering how to relate rather than on how to have sex – a great improvement on the current nonsense passing as sex education in our schools. At the end, all her heroes marry, too!)

There is a strong emphasis on the protective power of love, too. Harry's parents had sacrificed their own lives to save him when he was a baby, and the memory of their devotion not only inspires him in his own battles but is the source of much of his power. His mentor, Dumbledore, says: 'To have been loved so deeply, even though the person who loved us is gone, will give us some protection for ever.' Christians should be at home with such a notion. Likewise, the loyal acceptance of Harry by the Weasley family and by his closest chums, Ron and Hermione, demonstrates the strength of real friendship, and when that friendship is tested through misunderstanding – as it often is – it comes through stronger than ever.

It is this underlying quality that helps lift the books above the usual children's adventure story. For, although at one level this is a play on the British public school story of yesteryear – and one that uses all the stereotyped characters of both staff and pupils and that is told with the engaging humour of Anthony Buckeridge's *Jennings* stories – at another level it is mythic and instructive. As with all who seek their holy grail, Harry Potter is portrayed as a child of destiny who finds himself on a classical journey of self-discovery that mirrors so much of our own lives. Like all such travellers he is opposed by fierce adversaries, is challenged and trained by stern guardians and receives help from wise mentors – yet always he must face his deepest trials and make his crucial choices by himself. The drama runs high; we all want to know what will become of our hero, and we all know that this will be decided more by the quality of his character than by the skills that he has acquired along the way. Rowling's vivid world of the imagination, with its instant food, living portraits, magic sweets, passwords into secret places, crazy creatures, flying motor car, hordes of gold, aerial sports with intelligent balls, and spell-casting wands, has one other thing going for it. It appeals to our 'if only' daydreams. Contrived with ingenuity and humour (her word plays on names are wonderful) it is great escapism!

But is it more? Such stories might have been conceived without recourse to witchcraft. As we shall see later, although the author has brought her own unique imagination to bear on the theme, the plot is not particularly new.

Just as easily, Harry Potter could have discovered that he was a member of a special tribe or order who was destined to grow up as a liberator of the race. Once schooled in its culture and skills he could have faced his enemies with weapons that worked like magic but which were not in themselves magical. Advanced technology and the ingenuity of children could have provided all the necessary fun and sparkle along the way. The moral framework could have been just as clear and the imagination just as rich. There are many ways of telling such stories. So why use the world of witchcraft? Is there something more sinister going on, maybe some deliberate intention on the part of the author to lure children into the occult?

Some Christian fundamentalists seem to think so, and some have made fools of themselves, and done considerable harm to the credibility of the gospel, by quoting unsubstantiated, sensational nonsense drawn from X-rated satirical sources as though it were true. We should be ashamed of such folly; the world, as it often does, may malign us without integrity but we should not reply in kind.

Jo Rowling has stated that she writes for the sheer pleasure of it. A storyteller from childhood, she wrote the first *Harry Potter* book because it was the kind of story she wanted to write. The entire concept for the series came fully formed into her mind seven years before the publication of the first story. She says, 'I was going by train from Manchester to London, sitting there thinking of nothing to do with writing, and the idea came out of nowhere. I could see Harry very clearly: this scrawny little boy, and it was the most physical rush of excitement.'[3]

---

[3] Harry Potter and Me (BBC Christmas Special, British version), BBC, 28 December 2001.

Some Christian critics have immediately labelled this as occult impartation, akin to automatic handwriting, but in fact most authors of imaginative fiction have the same kind of experience. It is just the way the gift of storytelling works, and it is no more occult than an engineer envisaging, say, a Harrier jump jet or a Hovercraft. Neither of these novel machines were possible without the more or less total picture first coming to birth in the imagination of the inventor. Indeed, as we shall see in the next chapter, this ability to see complete stories and structures is one of those characteristics that demonstrates the fact that we are made in the image of God, who himself conceived an entire universe before creating it.

Rowling herself has made it clear that she does not believe in the magic found in her books. 'I don't believe in witchcraft, though I've lost count of the number of times I've been told I'm a practising witch. Ninety – let's say ninety-five percent at least – of the magic in the books in entirely invented by me.'[4] Nor has she any intention of seducing children into witchcraft. In one interview she is quoted as saying: 'I am not trying to influence anyone into black magic. That's the very last thing I'd want to do . . . My wizarding world is a world of the imagination. I think it's a moral world.'[5]

That doesn't let the *Harry Potter* books off the hook by any means. The author may not have sinister intentions, but her work does provoke some real questions about the shifting values of our contemporary culture, and the degree to which it reflects and contributes to those values is worth examining.

---

[4] Harry Potter and Me (BBC Christmas Special, British version), BBC, 28 December 2001.

[5] *USA Weekend*, 12–14 November 1999.

Some of those changes are positive and others quite disturbing, especially as they relate to our children. We need to understand what is being planted in their fertile imaginations and to ask what effect these things will have on their future lives. One thing is certain: they cannot grow up in a morally and spiritually neutral universe; that particular myth is well and truly scotched, and only fools and bigots believe otherwise. Equally certain is the fact that our children will be more influenced by what goes into their imaginations than by any series of logical arguments, however well presented those may be. It is a tragedy that many Christians become uneasy at this point, and so to this we must turn by taking a look at the phenomenon of imagination itself.

2
Just Imagine

It seems unlikely that earthworms engage in role-play games, or if they do they keep very quiet about it. Not so some others of God's creatures; many animals have an instinct to role-play that is vital to their survival, whether it be young stags practising head butts or lion cubs wrestling with one another in the pride. This is how they learn to defend themselves against predators, and how they develop their hunting skills. The family kitten with the ball of wool is learning how to hunt mice, even though it will probably only ever need to find its way to the bowl of Kittychunks in the kitchen.

However, all this is based on instinct, not imagination. Human children are different. Although, like the animals, we do play games that teach us basic survival skills, such as war-dances or Monopoly or Tomb Raider – depending upon the perceived needs of our particular social grouping – we engage in another level of play altogether, and it's because of who we are.

God has created us in his own image. This means we are the product of God's own imagination; what he saw in his mind, he made. It means, too, that we are a living image of what God is like; enter through the doorway of a human personality and you will find divine characteristics. These include the capacity for ideas, the use of language, the virtue of love – and imagination. Bearing this image is what makes us unique in creation and what drew the awed exclamation from the Psalmist, 'What is man that you are mindful of him...? You have made him a little lower than the heavenly beings and crowned him with glory and honour' (Psalm 8:4–5).

Being made in the image of the Imaginer, we have been given this unique and amazing ability to imagine for ourselves. We can form pictures, or images, in our minds and, by art and craft, and especially by words, convey those pictures to others so that they can see them in their own minds also. Here is a passage taken from one of my own works of fiction that I occasionally use with children when I visit schools to help them see how words build pictures and evoke moods:

> A pale golden mist lay across the damp fields and the early morning sun hung low on the horizon, a disk of crimson fire that flashed burnished highlights on young Sophie's blonde hair and kissed her honeyed skin with a blush of rose. Still warm from her slumbers, she opened the casement, smiled her serene smile, and breathed the cool air. It was sharp with the tang of early autumn, chilled cranberry sorbet all covered in wine. Rich russet leaves lay in curled flurries beneath the windless trees, and spiders' webs heavy with sparkling dew hung like tiaras on the dark brambles. Somewhere across the marshes a flock of Canada Geese rose in the dawn. Their faint mournful cry carried over the mists, and Sophie was filled with a soft sadness for the memories of summers past.

Creating characters and their roles takes us beyond survival games or mere amusement. Our stories and images enable us to reflect morally and spiritually about ourselves, and without them we have neither civilisation nor society. The arts – painting, music, drama, architecture, sculpture, and storytelling – are evidence of our humanity, the demonstration that we are made in the image of God. Monkeys don't build cathedrals, recite Shakespeare, or compose symphonies, and leaving aside the speculations of pseudo-science, nor will they in a million years.

This is why we humans cannot live without our stories, whether real-life or wholly imaginary, and why every society has its folklore complete with heroes and villains, adventures and exploits, laws and lessons – the more vivid and stirring the better. In Western culture, old favourites like Robin Hood and His Merrie Men teach us that government should be challenged if it becomes tyrannous, the rich have responsibilities to the poor, and the church should not be the indulgent lackey of the state. Very English, indeed, that!

The tales of King Arthur and his Knights profoundly shaped the notion of Christian chivalry, yet also reflected the uneasy interplay between Christendom and paganism in pre-scientific British culture. In these tales love, death and destiny weave their complex pattern in a world still trying to make up its mind about where the truth lies.

Cinderella reminds the downtrodden that miracles do happen and dreams can come true. How many girls hope for their Prince Charming as a result! We could go on: the Grimm brothers' fairy tales and Aesop's Fables with their moral instruction and cautions; *Huckleberry Finn* reflecting the uncertain transition of the American people into a nation; the plays of Shakespeare, or the novels of Dickens: *Oliver Twist* and *A Christmas Carol* both affirm the process of social reform initiated by the mid-nineteenth-century Christian revival.

These images and story games help shape not only our own character but the national, and increasingly the international character, so much so that today we can use a term like 'Western culture'. None of us escapes it: what we become in adult life is profoundly influenced by the images that we experience in our childhood, and the emotional and spiritual impact that those images have on our minds. Nor does it stop with the onset of adolescence. What we are as adults continues to be shaped by the tales of our times. As a result, we will more easily believe the picture story in our heads than some new doctrine or notion, however logically presented, that fails to trigger a more powerful image in our minds – an observation not lost on the advertising industry.

So, in a world saturated not only with images but with a vast number of stories that spark the picture house of the mind, it is essential that we weigh the values and the impact that these have, not only on ourselves but also on our children. We dare not shirk our responsibility to protect the weak and the vulnerable, and children in particular, who are at such a formative stage in their lives. Let their minds be bent and shaped the wrong way now, and the damage will prove difficult if not well nigh impossible to remedy. We cannot simply sit them in front of the television, or let them loose on the Internet; nor should we give them licence to read just anything they fancy simply because it is currently *cool*. Since when could we trust the media to set the moral and spiritual tone of the nation?

Plain common sense recognises that children should be protected from violent or sexually explicit images, but even here the drift is apparent and far too many children are exposed to images and information that are beyond their capacity to handle in a healthy manner. Too many of us tend to trust the government-appointed watchdogs and guidelines rather than make the effort ourselves. It's a dangerous laziness, for we live in a world that operates on a value system very different from our own and for whom the word 'imaginative', like the word 'art', is a justification for almost anything.

The Bible makes it clear that imagination is far from neutral. There is such a thing as vain, or futile, imagination. Paul the apostle reminds us in the context of Romans 1:21 that, be our idols of stone or steel, of sex or superstition or science, they have their origin in futile minds that have perverted the gift of God to serve lesser causes. One wonders, for example, what would have become of the theory of evolution had it been confined to the realm of genuine science. In all likelihood, it would have long been discarded as an inadequate explanation of origins. However, the vast investment in image-making by its proponents has lifted it to the level of myth and made it believable to the majority of the Western world – an apt fulfilment of Paul's words.

Since the world is given over to vanity, or futility, it is hardly surprising that much of what it produces, unless moderated by something better, consists of negative and cynical images. We have only to note the obsession with violence, death and eroticism in our film and television industries, so that even good plots nowadays contain obligatory blasphemy, killing and sex scenes. Why do they not contain an obligatory prayer, a gift to the poor, and assistance to someone in need? Because life's not like that? But, it is! Millions of people, and not just Christians, pray, give and assist others as part of their everyday lifestyle. But the writers and producers work to a different agenda, don't they?

We can't just blame the producers of our mainline commercial media. The Internet with its assertion of human autonomy is replete with millions of pornographic and violent images, many of which are just plain sick. This is another fantasy world that feeds a vain imagination. Likewise, much of our contemporary literature has followed the same cynical trend, and in so doing reduces our worth and experience to that of the dogs.

When it comes to media directed towards children there is considerably more restraint. Yet even here we find a world where Manga violence, monsters, horror and quasi-sexual imagery are rampant, where witchcraft and sorcery are commonplace, and where ghosts and ghouls provide the entertainment and excitement rather than anything better. We will comment later on the high levels of violence and horror in the Harry Potter stories.

Now, lest this seem too culturally negative, we do well to remind ourselves that not by a long way is everything bad. Since 'every good and perfect gift is from above, coming down from the Father of the heavenly lights' (James 1:17), non-believers are well capable of producing works of great moral and spiritual worth. Indeed, some of the greatest artistic and imaginative achievements have come from professing unbelievers. In the West, nonetheless, much of that has arisen from a culture that has been profoundly influenced and shaped by a Christian world-view. Delivering people from the superstitions of idolatry, the Christian faith has enabled the creative gift to explore beauty without fear and to reflect upon human nature without explaining our behaviour simply in terms of the caprice of the gods or the activity of demons. It is a legacy that we neglect at our peril. Lose God and we lose our humanity; lose our humanity and we become programmed machines, or the habitation of demons.

Seldom has there been a greater need for Christians to

engage positively and creatively in the imaginative arts. We do so in the great tradition of those who produced illuminated manuscripts, invented musical notation, designed the Sistine Chapel, built the cathedrals, painted the Dutch masters, wrote *Pilgrim's Progress*, shaped the heights of the English language with Tyndale's and the Authorised Versions of the Bible; we include in our ranks all the great names – Bede, Tyndale, Erasmus, Haydn, Bach, Handel, Rembrandt, Tolstoy – and many hundreds more, too numerous to mention – let alone the countless godly craftsmen and women who did and still do their work for the glory of God.

We must encourage the positive use of our imaginations. The apostle Paul urged us to think great thoughts: 'Whatever is true, whatever is noble, whatever is right, whatever is pure, whatever is lovely, whatever is admirable – if anything is excellent or praiseworthy – think about such things' (Philippians 4:8). This is no invitation to hide away from the harsh realities of life, and even less to daub everything with crosses and doves; nor does it mean we must never listen to secular music or read non-Christian books or watch a Hollywood film. What it does urge, however, is that we look at life from a positive and redemptive perspective. The Bible story does not begin with sin, rebellion and evil; it begins with a God of love who made a beautiful world that was shot through with goodness. Nor did the Fall spoil it all; God seriously limited the effects of evil and ensured that beauty would still remain and that we would aspire to find it. When history ends it will do so with the return of the most beautiful Man who ever lived and who will inaugurate a splendid new creation in which all evil is banished. Can you imagine it? You should!

The least we can do for our children is to ensure that they know the greatest story ever told, for this will provide them with the means by which to judge all other tales when they encounter them. The divine drama, as unfolded in the Scriptures, is not only full of great tales in their own right, but the impact of those stories on the imagination helps shape a healthy world-view and provide the moral inspiration that children need in order to discern between good and evil.

Of course, they will have to face the full impact of the world's images in the course of their lives and certainly as they grow into adulthood. No one can protect their children by hiding them away, and sets of rules or approved lists will do little more than make them either fearful in their imaginations or just longing to break the taboos to find out what is there.

This is the danger of treating the Bible merely as a set of theological propositions and proof texts, as some branches of the church are apt to do. The Bible is a story book, a true-story book, but none the less a narrative form through which God progressively reveals himself and his will for the human race. All our proof texts must be seen in the wider context of the narrative. Those truly steeped in the Bible will have allowed its images and stories to shape their minds into seeing as God sees. They will not simply quote chapter and verse but rather, guided by the Holy Spirit and in fellowship with others, will develop the art of true discernment.

Taking a text out of context and making it a pretext can allow us to prove anything we want from the Bible. It is a dangerous and ultimately unbiblical form of interpretation (or exegesis) of God's Word, and it produces the knee-jerk reaction of rigid fundamentalism that so discredits the gospel. In the case of *Harry Potter* the logic runs like this: 'It's about witches, the Bible says witches should be put to death. The author knows too much about witchcraft. She must be one herself. So. . .' Such views are ill-informed and are motivated far more by fear than by the love of truth. What our children need instead is to learn the true wisdom that comes from above, and to learn it in the narrative form that parallels the way in which they have to live their own lives.

It would be a grave mistake and a theological error to restrict our children's reading to the Bible, or even to just 'Christian' books. They need access to the wealth of good reading that we have available to us – books that inspire the imagination and encourage a positive and caring lifestyle. These don't have to be just nice stories. Indeed, we may do more harm than good by restricting their reading to books that fail to do justice to the realities of life. The Bible is never like that! Children do need to know about hatred and injustice, about suffering and disease, about conflict and victory, about hope and despair, about life and death. J K Rowling does not shrink from letting us face these realities in her books: 'I remain of the firm belief that we need our imaginary villains, the better to brace ourselves for the ones we need to fight in reality.'[1] How well she handles them is for our later consideration. What our children don't need is literature that is selfish and cynical at heart, or that encourages a pathological gloom about life before ever they have had a chance to appreciate its beauties.

Why recommend books in an age of television, film, computer games and Web-surfing? Simply because good books, like radio stories, stimulate the imagination far, far better than film or television can ever do. Words create images in our minds; whereas the televisual and cinematic

---

[1] *Bigbadread*, www.bigbadread.co.uk, 4 September 2006.

media merely give us someone else's pictures. Who has not been disappointed with a film rendition of a favourite book simply because the images projected on the screen are nowhere near as good as the ones in our heads? Whatever you hear to the contrary, the fact is that more people than ever before are curling up with a bit of processed tree and printer's ink and loving every minute of it. The book is far from dead!

Wise parents and teachers will encourage the imagination of the children in their charge. They will ask about the images that come into their heads. Some may seem silly or childish to us, but that is perhaps because we have settled into a way of looking at life that no longer allows for a freshness of approach. We should respect our children's own ways of seeing things and avoid the temptation to dismiss their ideas as foolish, otherwise they will learn never to indulge us with their secrets, and that is simply asking for trouble. I often do mind maps with children when I visit primary schools for story-writing classes. Once they are released, the fertility of children's imaginations is a constant source of amazement and instruction. The tale of a man with a thousand boots to put on his feet, dreamed up by one of our grandchildren during a long car journey, may have been wacky, but it led to all sorts of discussions about time and practicality and why it was probably best that God gave us just two legs!

How much should we protect children from the effects of their imaginations? That will depend to a large extent on the sensitivity of the individual child. However, some books, like some TV programmes, are simply not going to be good for them because the material is intrinsically evil. Others will be suitable only when a child has reached a sufficient stage of emotional development to handle the content. An underdeveloped mind will not be able to cope with the overloaded imagination. This is what often causes bad dreams and nightmares. This is a tension picked up in *Harry Potter*, as we see Dumbledore struggle to decide how much or how little to tell Harry, recognising that too much would overwhelm the boy.

If we find that our children are being disturbed, or if their behaviour pattern is being affected by what they have read, we should quickly censor any further involvement. We should also pray with them about whatever it is that is upsetting them. It is one thing to read about ghosts, it is quite another to be left with a ghost in the imagination. Thus Christian parents and teachers need to be sensitive in the way that they deal with the issue of heaven and hell. It is one thing to know the facts but quite another to embellish those facts with lurid images that go far beyond the Scriptures. For younger children, to know that heaven is where Jesus is, and hell is where he is not, is probably sufficient.

Many years ago we prayed for a girl who at too young an age had seen the 1930s version of *King Kong* (by far the scariest in our opinion). That night the gorilla had walked through her bedroom wall and entered her head. From that time onwards she had suffered from severe epilepsy, complete with the characteristic dip in the brain scan printout. Years later one of her parents brought her to our church, and we prayed for her deliverance. Her epilepsy disappeared and the brain scans returned to normal. Now I am obviously not suggesting that this is the cause and cure of all cases of epilepsy, but the point is, we do need to be aware of what is taking place in our children's imaginations, and we do need to be wise over what we allow them to read or view, lest they become prey to every opportunistic spirit and wind of doctrine that blows their way.

Sci-fi and fantasy are particularly powerful forms of literature since they invoke entire worlds of the imagination quite unlike our own. Fantasy also addresses the subconscious mind, especially if it is based on a mythic structure, as we will see in the next chapter. It has a great power for good, and also for evil. The *Harry Potter* stories fall into this genre of literature.

We will examine the good and bad points of these stories in the pages that follow, but suffice it to state right now that in our opinion the power and the darkness of the imagery, and the graphic and at times gory scenes, makes these unsuitable reading for most children below the age of ten. Parents of highly impressionable children may wish to restrict the books to an even later age, especially as the darkness and violence of the plots increase as the series progresses.

This is a matter of common sense. The author has, quite legitimately, determined that her characters should grow up, and that the subject matter should in consequence become more adult. These are books about teenagers, not about children, and from volume four on they are dealing with matters in a manner that is more appropriate for teenage readers than for nine-year-olds. As Rowling's theme darkens, parents with younger children will do well to decide when it is appropriate for their children to read the subsequent volumes and, when they do, to ensure that they discuss the subject matter with them.

It follows, too, that parents should be aware of, and discuss with teachers, what books are available in the school library and reading corner, and which ones are used as course work. Most teachers of worth are sympathetic to concerns pleasantly and politely expressed by parents and governors.

We must recognise, too, that the merchandising machine has been hard at work raking in the bucks. It is a fact of life that once a product or idea gains a sufficient profile, quantity and variety of product becomes more important than quality. Commercial interests pay scant regard to the morality of their products. The bottom line is everything. So, *Harry Potter* can appear harmlessly on a cereal packet but he may also become the sales icon for distinctly unhelpful role-play occult experimentation games. Common sense tells us not to ban the cereal packet but certainly to ban unhelpful merchandise and to set proper limits if we detect that our child is getting obsessively into *Harry Potter*.

One further area where parents and others need to exercise wisdom concerns the *Harry Potter* films. One of the differences between books and films is that books are to some degree self-censoring. Younger children are precluded both by their reading age and by subject matter that exceeds their education. In such cases the book is incomprehensible, or as the child is more likely to say, 'boring'. By contrast, film versions of books make the images and story line accessible to anyone who watches, and so require parents to decide whether they are appropriate material for their children.

Imagination is one of the finest gifts that God has bestowed upon us. All major scientific discoveries, all social and political reforms, come about because of its use. Martin Luther King's famous words say it all: 'I have a dream. . .' We should nurture and encourage our children to dream, to imagine a better world. With God's help, they may just go on to produce it.

3

The World Between Worlds

Human beings will persistently not accept that reality is limited to mortal, material existence. Whether couched in terms of the realm of the dead, or the world of spirits, or the gods of Olympus, or heaven and hell, from time immemorial we have believed that there is more to life than meets the eye, and no amount of left-brained rationalism will convince us otherwise.

Christians will wish to make the point that this is because the human heart retains its longing for God. In the words of King Solomon, God has 'set eternity in the hearts of men; yet they cannot fathom what God has done' (Ecclesiastes 3:11). Paul the apostle, speaking in Athens, declared that God set all humans in time and space 'so that men would seek him and perhaps reach out for him and find him,' adding, 'though he is not far from each one of us' (Acts 17:27). This tantalising concept of 'God most high and God most nigh' invites us both to worship the Mystery and to love the Friend – and either way he is much nearer than we think. In the words of an old hymnwriter, 'Tis only the splendour of light hideth Thee.'

Creation saturates our senses with the revelation of God within the boundaries of our mortality, but there are times when greater glimpses of glory and grace transcend those boundaries. The transfiguration of Jesus is a good example. One of the witnesses to this phenomenon, Peter, says , 'we were eyewitnesses of his majesty . . . We ourselves heard this voice that came from heaven' (2 Peter 1:16, 18). Such epiphanies take us to another realm and give us the opportunity to glimpse a farther shore, such as when the apostle Paul speaks of being 'caught up to the third heaven . . . to paradise' (2 Corinthians 12:2, 4).

The Bible also speaks about a sphere of strategic conflict, a spiritual battleground called 'the heavenlies', and suggests that this is a reality rather than simply the realm of religious imagination. If this is so then we should have little difficulty with the idea of parallel worlds or a 'pluriverse' of wheels within wheels. Indeed, arguably the founder of modern multi-dimensional fantasy is the apocalyptic writer of the Book of Revelation, the apostle John, though the antecedents go right back to Old Testament prophets like Daniel and Ezekiel. (It is pedantic to say that the pluriverse is really a universe because God made it all – a bit like saying that the different but interconnected worlds of India and Canada are both on planet Earth, as if we needed reminding!)

John's vivid imagery continues to haunt our imagination and profoundly affects our Western consciousness. We have only to think of Apocalypse, Armageddon, The Mark of the Beast, or The Four Horsemen for direct references, let alone films like *Terminator 2* that reflect the motif of Revelation 12. John's vision came about through an altered state of consciousness and his awareness of entering a parallel world – a world that he could only describe by means of images. 'I was in the Spirit,' he says. 'I looked, and there before me was a door standing open in heaven' (Revelation 4:1–2). His purpose is that we should see the drama of human conflict and its ultimate resolution on a broad and vivid canvas. Revealed is a war of the worlds, and we are called uncompromisingly to choose sides, with the profoundest consequences for our character and our destiny.

Novelists need an arena for their stories, some way of setting boundaries to the tableau, a plate for the meal, so that the tale may work. For a novel is not the whole history nor a limitless landscape, nor all the food in the kitchen. Traditionally this is done by use of bounded places such as the monastery, the country house, the palace, the village, the school or the island. Rowling uses the setting of Hogwarts School. More intensely psychological novels use a limited circle of relationships with little regard to geography – anything from a domestic couple to a squad of soldiers to a secret global network. It is the stuff of soaps and sitcoms, too.

Modern fantasy authors explore parallel worlds – those wheels within wheels that provide us with fascinating settings unbounded by convention or experience. Such 'distancing' provides a fresh way for us to reflect on our existence through the lives of players who may be like us or quite different, as with talking animals or mythical creatures like elves and dwarves. In many parallel-world tales what happens in one realm has implications for our own, a reminder perhaps that stories do more than entertain. Such tales can help us see beyond our own paradigms and learn otherwise overlooked truths.

Quantum theory suggests a scientific justification for parallel-world tales because it includes the possibility of multiverses or pluriverses operating in ways different from our own universe – and the fascinating thought that we might find ways of moving between these. However, the roots, as we have noted, are far older than modern theoretical physics. They are religious and particularly Judeo-Christian. For this reason such stories are more likely to carry subtexts, that is, to be multi-layered with meaning, and that is part of the appeal both to writers and to readers.

J K Rowling is using a parallel-world structure in the *Harry Potter* series. In this she stands in the tradition of writers as diverse as Lewis Carroll, George MacDonald, Beatrix Potter, George Orwell, William Horwood, J R R Tolkien, C S Lewis and many other science fiction and fantasy writers. Indeed, Rowling honours C S Lewis' evocative 'world between worlds', a wooded land of pools where to jump into any one of them is to discover another realm.[1] Rationally, Rowling sees this as a metaphor for a library, though Lewis had much more in mind. Nonetheless, like Lewis, Rowling's subtext is redemptive myth, of which more later. Suffice to say at this point that Harry Potter, through his trials and tribulations, will save himself from the bonds of Muggledom and bring deliverance from the bane of Voldemort. By the end of the sixth volume, following the death of Dumbledore, having been tried and tested in lesser conflicts, he understands this with cold and deliberate certainty.

Another of Rowling's subtexts is to attack the banality of bourgeois modernity and its limited rationalistic and materialistic horizons. She invites her readers to a world of fun, imagination and adventure and eternal values. John Granger writes:

> Not that these books don't have a biting satirical and sardonic edge! *Harry Potter* is a traditionalist broadside attack on the modern world and its absurdities. Rowling's traditionalism shows itself in her profound use of alchemical symbolism in

---

[1] C S Lewis, *The Magician's Nephew*, HarperCollins 1955.

every book and the medieval and magical setting of Hogwarts. She creates a technology free, virtue laden world in order to critique modernity's obsession with toys and neglect of everything meaningful. She fills this world with magic as a counter spell to break the materialist enchantment of our effeminate, one-dimensional culture. Harry is a Christian hero, and a masculine icon of the traditionalist, symbolic outlook to boot.[2]

This is a message that needs to be heard in a day when our education systems are so geared in the opposite direction and we are in danger of producing little more than trained operatives kept quiet by a diet of self-indulgent consumerism. It is a theme echoed, albeit with ladles of sentimental kitsch, in the film *Dead Poets Society*. Christians ought to champion imaginative education.

Along with this goes Rowling's dismissal of horoscopes and other trite folk culture superstitions. In this she goes so far as to suggest that even when the Divination teacher, Sybil Trelawney, produces what is taken to be a true prophecy, its fulfilment ultimately depended on the mere fact that Voldemort believed it. As Dumbledore says to Harry, 'The prophecy is significant only because you and Voldemort choose to make it so.' If you both choose to walk away, you could both live! That's the bottom line.

Likewise the tabloid journalist, Rita Skeeter, gets short shrift for her cheapskate sensationalism designed to titillate the bored masses. It seems even the world of wizardry can succumb to banality! Rowling's point is that life is much more serious; there are real powers, there is real conflict and the stakes are high. There is a powerful political subtext to these books, not of the simplistic kind, such as seeking to

---

[2] John Granger, 'The Christian Meaning of *The Chamber of Secrets*', http://www.george-macdonald.com/harry_potter_granger.htm

analyse them through the framework of a Marxist critique, but a depiction of the serious threat that fascism poses to our society.

Does Rowling have a deeper subtext, an intention to open children up to the world of witchcraft and the occult? Is she entertaining children into arcane knowledge in the hope that many will embrace it? The possibility is there but the evidence is lacking. Rowling herself consistently denies it, so much so that if she were to turn out to be a secret witch as some would have it, she would have shot her credibility to pieces. She acknowledges that as a child she enjoyed playing witches and wizards with her friends, but that was always in the context of playful mischief. Some may nod darkly at this and say, 'Aha, told you so,' but it is stretching the point. The child who insisted on being king of the castle does not grow up to be a preacher of monarchical megalomania, nor does the child taking the role of Tyrannosaurus Rex mature into leader of the Hannibal Lecter dining club!

That said, a distinction has to be made between the author's stated intention and the likely effects of an author's work, and although authors can hardly be blamed for the behaviour of their readers it will not do for an author wholly to disown responsibility. By creating a world of wizardry not far removed from ours, and overlapping it, she inevitably puts all things witchy on the agenda of children's minds. Top writers know what they are doing (though, to be fair, she was not a 'top writer' when she began). In spite of her claims that most of the material came straight from her head it is evident that Jo Rowling has, as one would expect, done her research very thoroughly. Sometimes the results are playful. At other times they are very serious indeed, as when, at the end of *The Goblet of Fire*, Voldemort undergoes a black-magic blood ritual to reincarnate himself. This material accords with genuinely occultic rituals.

Fantasy it may be, and not believed by the author herself, but make the subject fascinating, entertaining and accessible and you open wider the possibility that some will take it far more seriously than is healthy. Viruses may enter the body through perfectly pleasurable ways, and that, in our current climate, is a reasonable concern. Some children will confuse fantasy with reality, just like the boy with a sore head who tried to run through the barrier between platforms nine and ten at King's Cross Station! Common sense says that we must ensure that our children know the difference between fantasy and reality. Most do, but the lines can be blurred. As with so many potentially hazardous substances it is a case of 'use with caution'. Or find something more natural and environmentally friendly.

Those of a merely rational world-view will dismiss all this as a needless and laughable concern. Yet even at the level of rationalistic psychology it is recognised that attempts to manipulate people or events by paranormal means can become obsessive, ritualistic and pathological. This may lead to delusions, sleep disturbances, anti-social behaviour and compulsions. Those with a more enlightened world-view will recognise the additional possibility of people opening themselves up to malign forces, or spirits, with consequent self-destructive effects. Not exactly a sensible path to take!

Having said this, we must beware of being so jumpy about the occult that we lose our common sense and overlook some of the other very real battlefields.

It is very easy to make a certain type of Christian jump. Just say any of the following words: witch, wizard, magic, spell, crystal, cards, and they will start praying against it.

Use the words luck, fortune, chance and they will wish to correct your theology with the preferred word 'providence'. Point taken, but for such people the world is fraught with demons, and deception lurks at every turn. The *Harry Potter* adventures are for such a veritable viper's nest of evil.

While not wishing to minimise or trivialise the reality and the dangers of the truly occult, the bigger danger is that it may draw our fire away from the really important targets. Here are three of particular concern, though there are many more.

The first is the exposure of our children to a rapacious consumerism pumped out by the media that teaches them to measure their life, status and worth by the quantity and 'coolness' of their possessions. We need to call for a far better emphasis on the acquisition of spiritual and moral virtues, and to insist that our children are taught the real values of life. If Jesus is correct when he says, 'It is more blessed to give than to receive,' then we will do well to encourage service towards others, particularly those who are in need.

The second is to do with the premature sexualising of children in our society. Music, fashion, humour and current sex education programmes all impose an adult agenda of sexual awareness, allure and technique on children too young to appreciate the emotional commitment involved in sexual activity. It may be cool to be sexy, but not when you are a nine-year-old child. Cute it ain't. We need to fight for a better alternative to the disastrous 'sex is for recreation but use a condom' philosophy, however long it takes to change public opinion and public policy.

The third area of concern is the rise of Christianophobia and a pernicious misrepresentation of the Christian faith in our educational establishments, which reduces a vibrant global faith to an historical white Western curiosity and implies that all the church ever did was to wage war, censor progress, abuse cultures and burn witches at the stake. Little wonder children feel their innate faith undermined to the point where many grow cynical.

As a brief detour, we may note another contemporary writer who most certainly uses fantasy to perpetuate the misrepresentation of the Christian faith. Philip Pullman's *His Dark Materials* trilogy, consisting of *Northern Lights*, *The Subtle Knife* and *The Amber Spyglass*, is a pluriverse fantasy concerning the fortunes of Lyra, a misfit ward of an Oxford college who goes in search of her abducted friend. Unknown to her she is chosen to be the new Eve who will inaugurate the Republic of Heaven. Meanwhile, a war must be fought against the Kingdom of Heaven which is ruled by an arch evil known as 'God, the Creator, the Lord, Yahweh, El, Adonai, the King, the Father, the Almighty' and is called The Authority though is in fact only the Regent of the Ancient of Days, the latter being a pathetic being that finally dies with a sigh of relief. The wicked instrument of God is the Church, a vicious organisation that kidnaps children and mutilates them by cutting out their daemons, that is, their souls. Lyra herself is adept at using divination to find her way through this pluriverse landscape, and the tale culminates in a redemptive quasi-sexual act of love between pubescent children who then sacrificially decide not to see each other again for the good of the pluriverse.

I have given Pullman's work fuller treatment elsewhere,[3] but suffice it to say here that he writes an unabashed polemic against the Christian faith, or at least his parodied

---

[3] John Houghton, *A Closer Look at His Dark Materials*, Kingsway Publications 2004.

version of it, that uses many subtle and not so subtle devices to turn children from believing. In its place, Pullman offers a form of materialistic pantheism not far removed from C S Lewis' Materialist-Magician. 'If once we can produce our perfect work – the Materialist Magician, the man, not using, but veritably worshipping, what he vaguely calls "Forces" while denying the existence of "spirits" – then the end of the war will be in sight.'[4]

Pullman's work is pure Christianophobic propaganda, but when we return to *Harry Potter* we find no such militant agenda. Whatever else we may wish to level at Rowling's work, her subtexts are legitimate to her plot and the development of her characters. Indeed, there is no moral ambivalence or counter-Christian message in her exposé of the satanic figure Voldemort and his ways. In the *dénouement* of the first volume, the traitorous Quirrell boasts, 'A foolish young man I was then, full of ridiculous ideas about good and evil. Lord Voldemort showed me how wrong I was. There is no good and evil, there is only power, and those too weak to seek it.' This is pure Nietzsche, and given the renewed popularity of Friedrich Nietzsche's nihilistic philosophy over the past forty years, we welcome its clear renunciation by Ms Rowling. The pervasive influence of Nietzsche's philosophy is especially prominent in the American psyche, particularly through the influence of Freud and Jung. It is then surprising that some of the right-wing Christian fundamentalists have not been more supportive of Rowling's stance. Or does that beg a deeper question?

We cannot have yesterday's merely rationalistic world back. This is a rapidly changing culture, replete with worlds within worlds, where fantasy often conveys reality and

---

[4] C S Lewis, *The Screwtape Letters*, HarperCollins 1942.

what we sometimes perceive to be reality, is no more than fantasy. We must equip ourselves and our children to discern good from evil in this generation, and we must seize positively the cultural opportunity that a revived interest in the spiritual world presents for all who believe that 'the one who is in you is greater than the one who is in the world' (1 John 4:4). This is no time for hiding our heads in the sand or our lights under buckets. This is our journey, and we have a great story to tell to our fellow pilgrims.

4

The Mythic Journey

There is a primary principle that every true apostle and missionary understands: be it ever so corrupt, we must engage the indigenous culture rather than withdraw from it. Failure to do so guarantees that we shall lose the battle for the hearts and minds of men and women. A Christianity content to create its own subculture is doomed to fade into obscurity.

Engaging the culture means recognising and honouring good wherever we find it and yet being healthily critical of cultural evils. It means redeeming what can be redeemed, transforming what needs transforming and rejecting whatever is base and worthless. It is a proactive approach rather than a reactive one, so much so that it includes taking a lead in shaping the future direction of the culture. Christ is Lord of history, and every generation and culture is graced with opportunities to proclaim the gospel in terms that are both comprehensible and prophetic.

To understand the success of *Harry Potter* we must take a look at our contemporary culture. We are a generation of travellers, a motif that has revived the idea of pilgrimage or quest as a way of approaching the mystery of human existence. We are born and we live, and we die – but why?

What is this journey for, especially if we have a less than perfect start in life? Stories help us to reflect vicariously on the course and meaning of our own lives, and the best stories always involve journeys undertaken by unlikely and reluctant heroes. Their perils, their acquired wisdom, their battles, their courage inspires us; their triumph gives us hope as we face our own trials.

The kind of journey that makes for a compelling story in any given generation or culture is determined by the then current big adventure. For example, when colonisation of the Mediterranean islands was the big adventure we had Ulysses and the stories of Sinbad the Sailor, tales of gods and demons and magic – for the traveller's world is always dangerous outside the comfort of his familiar gods and gurus. The Crusader knights and the colonisation of Europe and the Middle East inspired the British high romance we call the legend of King Arthur. In the revitalised religious age of Puritan spirituality it was John Bunyan's *Pilgrim's Progress* (1678) that caught the imagination.

Later in history, Western exploration led to the great tales of adventure on the high seas, where strange cultures and unknown landscapes made for exciting reading, as we explored and exploited new continents. *Gulliver's Travels* by Jonathan Swift (1726) is a good example of a fantastic story satirically exposing truths about ourselves and society.

The Victorian journey was economic; hence, the rags to riches odyssey of Charles Dickens's *Oliver Twist* (1838). The theory of evolution gave literary birth to a search for lost worlds where evolution was at an earlier stage of development, as in *The Land that Time Forgot* by Edgar Rice Burroughs (1918). By the 1960s the journey had become sexual, spawning among many others the salacious *Emmanuelle* books and films. With the opening up of space travel it was *Star Trek* with its famously infamous split infinitive, *to boldly go...*

So what of today? We have explored the planet and few places are now more than a couple of days' journey away. Space travel is on hold awaiting further technological advances. The outward journey is over, but the exploration of the mind and the spirit has scarcely begun.

Today's great adventure has to do with the life within and beyond the physical. In a self-conscious age, the stories of today reflect our search for inner meaning. *Harry Potter* is of this kind, with its dark Jungian archetypes, its revisiting of ancient mythologies and its search for redemptive meaning in personal trials. It is cast understandably in the world of wizardry because our society believes that the only way you can undertake the inner journey is through revisiting paganism, or at least by escaping from mere materialism.

This is a real rebuke to a church that has largely failed to be a source of true spirituality to this generation. Instead we have presented ourselves as a formal religion of oppressive rituals and rules and redundant, reactionary values. The charismatic wing has fared little better. People consider it to be happy-clappy, culturally escapist and locked into 1970s existentialism, deeply paranoid about anything spiritual outside of its own cultural straitjacket.

The real challenge of *Harry Potter* and similar stories is not to expose how much occult-sounding material we can find in the books – there is quite a bit – nor to accuse the author of sinister intentions – she is a product of her age – nor to bemoan the damage it will do to children's minds – it may leave an unhelpful aftertaste; it is instead to understand the nature of the quest in our generation and to guide people to Jesus who is the one true path. The current journey involves searching for spiritual meaning, grappling with the mystery of evil, recognising the limits of the world of materialism, attempting to sift truth from falsehood, exploring integrity and motives, discovering the redemptive power of love. Surely we should be at home in such territory? Recast our unchanging gospel in these terms, be unafraid to use the neo-pagan idioms to our advantage, use storytelling as our means of conveying truth, and we might begin to make an impact on this generation.

Harry Potter's own journey is imperfect. He makes mistakes. Even his chief mentor turns out to be fallible. No one gives him all the answers, so he learns by process. If we are to help today's seekers, it is no use giving them stock abstract answers to questions they have yet to face or to ask. Instead, we must walk their journey with them, all the time pointing the way to Jesus, drawing upon and applying examples from life and not worrying too much about empirical schemes of theology.

Nor is Harry's journey easy and triumphalist. People die; Cedric Diggory is callously murdered by Voldemort simply because he was in the wrong place at the wrong time. He is no hero and we are forced to face the apparent meaninglessness of death and evil. When Harry and Dumbledore escape from the cave with what they take to be one of Voldemort's horcruxes (objects in which he has secreted part of his soul), bitterness is laden on bitterness when Dumbledore dies and the horcrux turns out to be a fake. We are not allowed a divine intervention, *deus ex machina*, to magic away our problems. The challenge, and one that Christians should be happy with, is for Harry to grow as a person by learning lessons of forgiveness (he even extends to Voldemort an invitation towards remorse), overcoming personal fear and dealing with his adolescent rages, until he is ready to fulfil his ultimate calling.

So, where is today's cultural pilgrimage taking us? For some it is no more than a consumer trip to the shopping centre for a bit of retail therapy, but many others are turning elsewhere.

No stories have greater power on the imagination than those built around what we call mythic structure. It is sometimes called the Hero's Journey. Such stories include the old legends of King Arthur, and Odysseus, and the voyages of Sinbad. Modern examples that follow the same pattern include *The Lord of the Rings* and *The Wizard of Oz* and *Star Wars*.

It is a pattern that goes something like this: A very ordinary person is called to make a heroic journey to save the world. He accepts the call reluctantly, not believing the special secret about his real identity. A wise mentor appears and gives him advice. He crosses the threshold into the realm of high adventure and soon faces stern guardians who have to be bribed, impressed or silenced. There he finds magic weapons to help him. A series of trials follows, in which he will be helped by various allies. There will also be a trickster – an ambivalent character who will constantly test the hero but whose true motives are unknown. Somewhere in the background will lurk a sinister shadow. Eventually, the hero must undergo the supreme ordeal which he must face alone. There he will be tested as to his character – either by encountering a goddess figure, or by sacrificially making atonement with the Father, or by undergoing elevation to divine status. If he comes through the test he will obtain the elixir of life. The hero must then return to his own people. This is not easy and he might flinch at the journey. However, help will come, often by means of flight, and the hero will return to his own world. When he does so, he will be master of both realms, for his journey has proved to be one of self-discovery, and it has made him a man. In the words of Aldous Huxley, 'The man who comes back through the Door in the Wall will never be quite the same as the man who went out.'[1]

Mythic stories may or may not be based on historical truth, but they contain profound truths about human existence, and therein lies their power. We are all on a journey called life; from the ordinariness of childhood, we must face the trials and uncertainties of growing up. Along the way we will make some friends and face some enemies. We will master some skills and face our shadowy fears. At some point we may encounter a decisive challenge to our future. Many fail at this encounter and they pay the price, which is to enter adulthood emotionally trapped in adolescence. Nowhere is this more apparent in our society than in sexual relationships. So many people bowing to sexual allure outside of marriage become incapable of sustaining a marital relationship in adult life. Instead, like pubescent teenagers, they keep 'falling in love' without ever passing the test that enables them really to love as only a grown-up can.

Whatever the test, and however the test is framed, those who succeed are rewarded with emotional adulthood and, be it as mundane as earning a living and raising a family, they make their contribution to the good of society. For most of us, better to be a little hero than no hero at all.

Mythic tales help us live out our journey vicariously; that is, we see ourselves and learn through someone else's experience. In the success of the hero we find hope for our own uncertain path. We desperately want Frodo Baggins to cast the ring into the Cracks of Doom, because if he fails, what hope is there for the rest of us? If Frodo cannot defeat evil,

---

[1] Aldous Huxley, *The Doors of Perception*, Flamingo 1994.

will evil prove to be the stronger force after all? Similarly, we need Harry Potter to overcome the evil that is Voldemort.

This is how we face our inner terrors and dream our dreams. If the myth is doing its job it will inspire us to higher ideals and teach us its morals. Its ancestral archetypes – those ancient figures of fairy tales and enchantment – touch us deep inside; the metaphors and symbols fire our imaginations, so much so that they become the unconscious foundations of our lives. Such myths shape our value system and our world-view, and they shape who we will become.

It is at once obvious that the *Harry Potter* books are based on mythic structure. Each volume in itself is a mini-myth, but each is part of the larger myth of the ongoing plot. Harry the hero, like Dorothy in *The Wizard of Oz*, enters a parallel world. There he begins his dark journey to face the shadow in his past, to deal with both the blessing and the curse of his origins. Dumbledore is his wise though flawed mentor, and Ron, Hermione and Hagrid are among his allies. McGonagall is a gatekeeper; Snape is the trickster (and Wormtail before him); and Voldemort the shadow. Shapeshifters abound. Each of the seven volumes takes us closer to the ultimate showdown until it resolves when Harry is given the choice of hallows or horcruxes, ultimate power or the destruction of evil. In choosing the latter he finds redemption and brings peace to the world.

Because Rowling uses this mythic structure, the *Harry Potter* series is capable of exercising a profound influence on young minds. The question is whether the influence will be for good or for ill.

For many Christians the answer is simple: ban myth altogether; the word is too closely associated with falsehood, and such stories are too dangerous and disturbing. Give us safe, logical facts, solid scientific proof texts, systematic theology, and the 'real' stories of the Bible.

The concern is understandable, but wrongly placed. First, myth, in this context, means anything but falsehood. It is a true-story pattern that is modelled on the realities of life. Second, the safe, logical, unimaginative approach is not biblical. God is good, but he is never 'safe'. The Bible itself is a narrative that is largely based on a mythic structure. We should expect this, since God's word is truth and must relate to the realities of our human experience. It also contains the mythic (not mythical) exploits of characters like Joseph, David, and above all, the life of Christ. As we read the Gospels we discover all the key elements of myth portrayed in the greatest story ever told. Little wonder it should be such a captivating and compelling story. The Holy Spirit himself has inspired the form as well as the words!

I want to avoid any confusion at this point: the mythic form of the Scriptures allows us to call it myth but it is not make-believe, folk legend or fiction. These events really happened in our space-time continuum, they are historically true and culminated in the Word becoming flesh and dwelling among us, full of grace and truth (John 1:14), and the Bible writers are careful to ensure that we understand this. 'We did not follow cleverly invented stories when we told you about the power and coming of our Lord Jesus Christ, but we were eye-witnesses of his majesty' (2 Peter 1:16). When the Bible speaks as if historically true, we take it that it is.

The point of the incarnation and of all the rest of the Bible narrative is that God reveals himself through the story of people's lives. We do well to remember this, because much of our failure to communicate the gospel effectively in our post-modern world is a failure to recognise the importance of telling the story. Yet Paul himself, the most 'theological' of writers, drew constantly from the narrative of the Old Testament as well as from the life of Christ. The book of Romans, for example, cannot be understood without knowing the heroic journey of faith lived out by Abraham. How tragic that we should reduce this story to a few proof texts on the subject of justification by faith. Neat, logical, uninspiring; people go away without a narrative to fire their imaginations, and little wonder then that a vivid film, or even a soap opera, can wipe away the neat list of facts presented by the preacher *quod erat demonstrandum*. Which is perhaps why we feel it necessary to deliver the same thing in a different wrapping the next week!

In truth, our down-playing of the imagination and our obsession with linear logic owe more to the rationalism of the Enlightenment than to the Scriptures. Yet even science depends upon the imagination and upon stories for its progress. The clockwork universe, the big bang theory, the theory of evolution; all the science developed around such notions is based on images and narratives – and not necessarily true ones, either!

So, accepting that the Bible is a mythic narrative, should we stick to that alone? At least we can trust the word of God! While we should certainly steep ourselves and our children in the Scriptures, we should recognise two scriptural truths. First, God bestows common grace on all of humanity. So passionate is God about reconciling the world to himself that he accustoms us to his character through the many blessings of creation and culture alike. The world is littered with clues that point us unerringly in the direction of Christ. 'Great are the works of the Lord; they are pondered by all who delight in them' (Psalm 111:2); 'You open your hand and satisfy the desires of every living thing' (Psalm 145:16). God 'himself gives all men life and breath and everything else. From one man he made every nation of men, that they should inhabit the whole earth; and he determined the times set for them and the exact places where they should live. God did this so that men would seek him and perhaps reach out for him and find him, though he is not far from each one of us' (Acts 17:25–27).

Second, God uses unbelievers in his purposes, be they Balaam's ass, the pagan king Cyrus, 'my anointed', or the writers that Paul quotes on Mars Hill. This has led Christian thinkers like C S Lewis and many others to acknowledge that pagan writings can and do contain elements of truth that help us in our journey towards salvation. *Lord of the Flies*, for example, is one of the most powerful expositions of the reality of the fall of man and of the corruption of sin. *Terminator 2* is a vivid portrayal of the relentlessness of sin, the need for a saviour and the necessity of a sacrifice to destroy evil, with much of its plot line reflecting the symbolism of Revelation 12. The *Harry Potter* stories remind us of the redemptive power of sacrificial love.

If we accept the power and place of mythic stories, not only for their insights into the mystery of human existence but also because of their common grace potential to guide us in our search for reality, then we must judge such tales not just for historical accuracy or literary integrity but for their psychological, moral and spiritual accuracy, too.

It is impossible to characterise mythic tales as simply good or bad. Always there will be a mixture and we will need to exercise our own discernment. *The Lord of the Rings*, for instance, would rate highly with many Christians because of its fine moral tone and redemptive pattern. Yet it is also ultimately depressing; the golden age is past, the future mundane, and the notion of the afterlife is shrouded in the mists of uncertainty. These are hardly Christian notions!

We should certainly look for redemptive patterns in stories; good must win in the end, and where it doesn't then the reasons must be apparent. In the great Bible story of Saul and David, the reasons for Saul's failure are made clear, as they are, too, for David's victories and his shortcomings. Cynical tales would simply put it down to luck, and that is certainly the case with the interactive books and DVDs where the reader fights the enemy with no sense of moral superiority and learns nothing except that he was lucky to survive this time. Such stories truly are best left on the shelves. Certainly, it is made clear that many of Harry Potter's failings are due to his own folly, immaturity, impetuousness and anger. However gifted he might be, he must learn to make the right decisions. Dumbledore makes it clear that character is more important than ability, or birth.

The *Star Wars* myth, while containing many good elements, raises another kind of issue – that of world-view. In the case of *Star Wars* it is a Taoist/Buddhist view of reality where a yin/yang Force can be tapped into for good or ill, depending upon your personal predisposition. Such a view is in flat opposition to the Bible, and those Christians who likened the Force to the Holy Spirit could hardly have been more wrong. Many of our questions about *Harry Potter* are to do with the world-view portrayed by the author.

What if those myths contain elements of magic and enchantment? This is a prominent feature in the *Harry Potter* stories and one that in itself has been sufficient for some Christians to avoid the books. Do those same Christians also avoid the enchanting tale of *Cinderella* with her fairy godmother and magic pumpkin coach, or *Snow White and the Seven Dwarves*?

We need to distinguish between magic performed as a serious exercise of power and magic as a storyteller's symbol for life and transformation. In the case of *Cinderella* it is clearly the latter; her inner goodness in spite of her ill-use, her higher aspirations, her hopes and dreams, are rewarded by a magical experience that changes her life. We should not be afraid of this use of the term and when the teenager says, 'Jesus is magic!' he is quite right!

The issues are far more serious when it comes to manipulative magic. In real life the Bible condemns sorcery and all those who engage in the magic arts, whether they be the Egyptian magicians in the time of Moses, or the Babylonian magicians in Daniel's day, or the sorcerers in Israel, or any others. Revelation 22:15 bans such from the city of life: 'Outside are . . . those who practise magic arts.' At the heart of this kind of magic is a way of doing life without reference to God; a belief that we can manipulate the forces or the demons in order to better ourselves or others.

This is a form of idolatry. It is all very well for those who practise so-called 'white magic' to claim that they have no malice in their rituals compared to those who do 'black magic', but that is missing the point. Ritual magic itself is wrong, irrespective of the claimed motives of its practitioners. To steal from a neighbour to help someone in need may be a more noble motive than undisguised thievery, but it doesn't justify stealing. There are more legitimate ways of aiding a needy cause.

In *Harry Potter*, we have two elements running side by side: a comic one where the author, in a Disneyesque fashion, parodies the classic stereotypes of magic, and another darker element where magic is used as a weapon by both the good guys and the bad guys. While we may accept that the lessons in trivial spell-casting are a humorous parallel to learning general sciences in the real world, we cannot avoid the connection between this and the use of magic as a means of control and intimidation; one surely leads to the other in these books. Such a use in our world, even for good purposes, is unacceptable. Yet in the *Harry Potter* books there is an overlap between the two realms. It is unavoidable that Harry will use magic in the non-wizard world and, in fact, he does so on his aunt and uncle and their son, Dudley. Because they are portrayed as such revolting creatures we are led to approve Harry's actions on a 'serves them right' basis.

The magic in *Harry Potter* is not magical or enchanting in the fairy-tale sense, and the good stuff is not a symbol for life. These are sombre books about the exercise of power rather than personal transformation, serious stuff to do with the conflict between good and evil. It would be foolish to suggest that every reader of these books will be tempted to become a magician; but it is equal folly to imagine that no one will. At least some will try to use spells either as a defence against people or events that threaten them, or as a form of malice or revenge against others.

Christians have a better answer to both these situations. For those who are afraid, we recommend prayer to the living God whose perfect love casts out fear. For those who are vindictive, we recommend repentance from the sin of not loving their neighbour.

The rising interest in magic is not accidental. None of us can live long for scientific materialism alone. Our lives cry out for meaning, for enlightenment, for spirituality. Historically, that has been found, to use C S Lewis' phrase, in the 'deeper magic' of the cross of Christ, 'the Lamb slain from the creation of the world'. This is the truly old religion, not the paganism which arose as a futile substitute for the true knowledge of God after the expulsion of Adam and Eve from the garden of Eden. However tentatively Western man sets out on the road back to spirituality, he will sooner or later be faced with a fork in the road where he must choose to 'know the mystery of God, namely, Christ, in whom are hidden all the treasures of wisdom and knowledge' (Colossians 2:2–3); otherwise he will descend into witchcraft.

5
Talking of Witches

Paranoia is frightening! The trouble with a conspiracy theory is that to deny it is to confirm it. Surely the greatest deception is to appear innocent! It's a point well made by Arthur Miller in his play *The Crucible*, where he reminds us that paranoia can make witches out of any one of us. In his explanation of the phenomenon, which he calls 'daemonism', Miller suggests that a combination of disappointed hopes, inexplicable failures and superstitious fear gives rise to the need to find scapegoats rather than to look for more rational and responsible explanations for our ills. His warning is well founded, and Christians as well as governments are wise to take note; they may have been grossly exaggerated, but we are still living down the evil legacy of those medieval witch-hunts.

Witch-hunting is a sign of insanity. Driven by fear, the obsessive witch-hunter is most truly mad for – as G K Chesterton pointed out – the madman has not lost his reason, he has simply lost everything else except his reason, and that becomes the obsession of his life. If only we can rid the world of capitalism, or communism, or Christianity, or weapons of mass destruction, or international terrorism – or witches – then everything will be fine. No it won't. It's bad enough when governments do it, but when the world sees Christians making knee-jerk reactions to anything they don't like it concludes that our faith is not only shallow, but mad and dangerous.

Paul reminds Timothy, 'For God has not given us a spirit of fear, but of power and of love and of a sound mind' (2 Timothy 1:7 NKJV). Robust faith will not see demons under every rose bush, nor will it be blown around by the latest obsessional fads of our tragi-comic culture. The church of Jesus Christ across the globe daily takes on far greater obstacles than the 'witchcraft in Harry Potter' and overcomes them by the word of God and the blood of the Lamb – often at the cost of heroic self-sacrifice and with a rough-hewn nobility of character that puts Christians' cowardly opponents to shame. Truly, 'the world was not worthy of them'. Let us be known for our faith, not our fear, and if we have to find a right cause for which to die, be sure that *Harry Potter* isn't one of them.

All that said, *Harry Potter* is about active witches and wizards. Harry is a wizard and his parents are a wizard and a witch. We don't have to go hunting for witches – in this case, they are intrinsic to the plot. It is, then, perfectly legitimate for us as morally and spiritually responsible people to make an assessment of the witchcraft theme in these stories. To do so, we must look at the role of the witch in literature and folklore, and the reality of witchcraft in the world today.

Perhaps the most subtle and subconscious literary use of the witch is to represent the dark side of motherhood. In this instance the witch figure is often a shapeshifter, and may alternate between appearing both as a figure of compassion and as a tyrant; for it is in the power of a mother to provide nurture and protection but also to deny the same, either out of caprice or in order to force the child to grow up. In psychological terms this use of the witch motif refers back to the time of a child's weaning and to those apron-string ties by which a child is both protected by a mother but also subject to her will. In mythic tales, the hero overcomes the tyrant's control and becomes an adult able freely to choose his own destiny. In real life, once having released ourselves from the apron strings, we can then love our mothers by free choice. Such a usage can be seen reflected in the legends of *King Arthur*. There is more than a touch of this in the portrayal of the Virgin Mary in Mel Gibson's film *The Passion of the Christ*.

It might be observed that Harry's mother, while inspiring him by her sacrificial love, also represents a demand for him to follow in her footsteps. Harry is mature when he reaches the point where he can choose of his own will to accept or to reject his mother's path. Only then is he truly free.

Closely allied to this usage, and perhaps appealing more to girls, is the witch as representing the fear of the future, particularly for those who have lost one or both of their parents. The wicked stepmother becomes the archetypal image of the witch because she exercises power without love over the child's life and is herself often jealous of the child's youth, beauty and claim to her father's affection. Nowhere is this better portrayed than in *The Wizard of Oz*. *Snow White and the Seven Dwarves* demonstrates a similar usage, and, in both instances, with the help of friends the heroines discover the inner resources that they need to overcome their fear. Of the older stories, *Hansel and Gretel* is probably the most powerful tale of the witch representing archetypal fear.

Related to the debunking of fear is the comic usage of the witch, as in *The Sorcerer's Apprentice* and in the old sitcom

Bewitched. Here witches are fallible, human like us, their spells mostly go wrong, and even if they do work there is probably another explanation for why they appear to do so. Laughter is a great antidote to fear – a lesson we do well to learn and one that Harry Potter is encouraged to grasp, also. When boggarts (representing their deepest fears) attack the children they are encouraged to use the spell *Ridikulus* and to imagine something really funny, like your worst enemy with his trousers falling down. It's a good piece of pop psychology.

Occasionally the witch can be a redemptive figure, as in *Cinderella* where the fairy godmother magically produces beauty from ashes in a classic Christian 'love found, love lost, love found again' romance.

The witch or wizard may also be a representation of wisdom, as with Merlin in the tales of King Arthur, or Gandalf in *The Lord of the Rings*. This traces back to the original meaning of the word 'occult', which referred to the academic study of esoteric mysteries needing an explanation, rather than to participating in séances and the like. In this sense, too, the witch can be an instructor. Curses work because people have committed folly. This might be an error of morality or a failure of common sense. Either way, it is human error that gives ground for the spell to work. Tommy playing with matches might well allow the fire-witch to burn the house down! Albus Dumbledore clearly fulfils this wisdom-sourcing role in Harry Potter's life.

The witch may, of course, be a symbol for genuine evil, indeed for Satan himself, as is the case in *The Lion, the Witch and the Wardrobe*, where malice, manipulation and magic combine with deception to create a monstrosity that expresses the reality of spiritual evil personified. Similarly the psychopath, Voldemort, is the satanic figure in *Harry*

Potter. In C S Lewis' tale, only a redemptive sacrifice can overcome the devil, and the parallel with Christ's death and resurrection is easily drawn. Harry Potter makes a similar sacrifice, going like a lamb to the slaughter, though in his case he does not seem to die so much as to have a threshold near-death conversation with Dumbledore before returning to the fight. Whatever the hints, it is not intended to be an exact parallel to the resurrection of Christ. Having won through, Harry assumes a perfectly normal family life within his wizarding community. This is in stark contrast to Harry's final understanding of resurrection as the gateway to the next life, not a return to this one.

The other popular usage of the witch today is the political one, where witches engage in a battle for power using superhuman powers of psychological and physical manipulation. Such a use includes the non-occultic shapeshifters like *Superman* and super-heroes in general, as well as *Batman* and *The Invaders*, the latter a thinly disguised anti-Communist series if ever there was one! It also includes localised and more witchy manipulators like *Lizzie Dripping* and *Buffy the Vampire Slayer*. The *Harry Potter* stories include much of this kind of witchcraft. In all these cases, ordinary mortals are at the mercy of the bad witches and can only be saved by the intervention of the good witches. We shall return later to the implications of this view.

All this is a far cry from real witchcraft, the history of which can be traced back biblically to that associated with the fertility cults of Canaan and the magicians of Egypt and Babylon. So dangerous was this occult activity considered to be that under the Law of Moses the death penalty was prescribed: 'Do not allow a sorceress to live' (Exodus 22:18); 'Let no-one be found among you who sacrifices his son or daughter in the fire, who practises divination or sorcery, interprets omens, engages in witchcraft' (Deuteronomy 18:10).

Before we use this text to start burning innocent eccentrics, herbalists and nonconformist Christians, let's understand what this really means. The Bible has no word for witch or witchcraft in its original Hebrew and Greek languages. Instead, it uses descriptive words like mutterer or singer of spells, lot-caster, consulter of the dead, provider of talismen, reader of omens, understander of secrets, possessor of python spirit. Much of this activity both fed on and induced fear, and its nurturing of superstition was in direct opposition to faith in God. Serious as this was for the future of the nation and the redemption of the world, there was more.

We are talking here of serious occult practices, decidedly dark magic that opened people up to the reality of demon possession. This was more than a matter of superstitious fear ruling people's lives; it also engaged them in sexual immorality, idol worship, gross child abuse and child sacrifice. Little wonder that the Mosaic Law sought to ban such activities. Indeed, it was a failure to heed those instructions that led the Israelites into eventual captivity. Essential to a belief in monotheism and the morality that flows from it is a renunciation of all forms of occult activity. Finally shaking off their polytheism, the post-captivity Jews were able to pave the way for the coming of the Messiah and to make possible the spiritual liberation of the whole world.

For this reason, the New Testament is no less adamant that witchcraft has to go. While it does not call for the death penalty, and indeed offers instead salvation to witches who repent (e.g. Simon Magus in Acts 8:9–24, and the Ephesian believers in Acts 19:18–20), nonetheless the unrepentant are among those consigned to the second death (Revelation 21:8).

This does not mean that Christians should assist with the first death! True, blanket accusations of Christian witch-burning are grossly exaggerated, both in terms of the purported numbers and the suggestion that they were burned alive (most were not), but that some took place in the name of the faith is undeniable. The issue is complicated by historical factors, but we can state unequivocally that the biblical answer to witchcraft is the free proclamation of the gospel, not the stake.

Surprisingly, Rowling takes a rather frivolous approach to witch-burning. *The Prisoner of Azkaban* opens with a quote from Bathilda Bagshot about medieval fears of witchcraft, claiming that 'on the rare occasion that they did catch a witch or wizard, burning had no effect whatsoever'. Instead, the victim would perform a Flame-Freezing charm and then 'pretend to shriek with pain while enjoying a gentle, tickling sensation'. Maybe she intends the message that witch-burning is as futile as it is erroneous.

True followers of Christ have a better answer to witchcraft. Jesus came to reveal a loving heavenly Father who is not far from any one of us, and who is a very present help in time of trouble. His ministry on earth was not only compassionate, it was immensely powerful. When we read the life of Christ we enter a world where inner demons are vanquished, the sick are healed, miracles abound, the powerless are given hope and, through knowing Christ, the door to the spiritual Holy of holies is flung wide to welcome people into communion with the mystery of God himself.

If that were not enough, the ascent of Christ to the right hand of the Father not only set him above all other spiritual and mortal beings in the universe but heralded the outpouring of the Holy Spirit upon his church. The work that Jesus began, he continues through his people. All across the world the proclamation of the good news brings peace and confidence regarding the future. Angels intervene, demons still flee at the name of Jesus, the sick continue to be healed, the bereft find solace, the poor begin the process of transforming their lives, mercy is ministered to millions. If Christians withdrew their goodwill, surely society would collapse overnight.

True, none of this is an easy path, but it is the path to eternal life, and better that than the tragic alternative. The living word of God proclaimed in prophetic power, and exemplified in transformed lives that call on the name of Jesus, is the greatest 'spell' of all; the priestly celebration of the Lord's Supper by believers recalls and makes present a 'holy magic' that renders all other sacrifices null and void; the apostolic authority of the name of Jesus Christ on the lips of God's people declares that there is one Lord and one alone, who will one day return to judge the living and the dead.

Unlike mere religion, there is no hierarchy of merit among true believers; the lowliest Christian may pray with the authority of Christ. The gifts of the Holy Spirit are tools granted even to the apprentices of faith. The least recognised are seated with Christ in the heavenly places, 'far above all rule and authority, power and dominion, and every title that can be given' (Ephesians 1:21). We have a better way. Who needs witchcraft and its pale substitutes?

Evidently, many think they do. Humans want for supernatural help; of that there is little doubt. For all the wonders of modern science and medicine, we remain vulnerable creatures beset by fears and uncertainties, subject to accidents and ills and knowing no more of the future than we did a thousand years ago. Christians may declare that supernatural help comes 'from the Lord, the Maker of heaven and earth' (Psalm 121:2), and not from the hills upon which we make our futile offerings or from which we hope to draw on some supposed earth magic, yet in practice the Western church appears to be powerless, lacking the spirituality that people crave, and failing to address the real issues in their lives. Despairing of a materialistic church, people in need are increasingly likely to turn to a witch rather than to a saint. Indeed, it seems easier to believe in UFOs and extra-terrestrials than in angels.

There are reasons to believe that the profoundly evil side of witchcraft flourishes today and that it involves ritual killing and gross human degradation, much of it well outside the law of the land, let alone the law of God. Much more popular, however, is middle-class ecological paganism. This is the stuff of women's magazines and evening classes, of correspondence courses and 'Mind, Body, Spirit' sections in bookshops; it is the world of discreet covens practising their rituals and making their offerings, networking for peace and healing through astral projection, chanting their mantras and, as latter-day animists, contacting the elemental spirits of nature.

Closely bound up with all this is the New Age movement with its emphasis on Gaia, the Mother Earth, and the discovery of the god within. This is little more than a return to pantheism through a variety of techniques borrowed from across the world and westernised to become another form of consumerism.

Meanwhile, at the level of popular culture, millions indulge in the superstitious ritual of their daily horoscope, carry lucky crystals, dabble in séances and Ouija boards and much else besides. Witchcraft, the desire to manipulate our destiny and the destiny of others, has seldom been more prevalent.

For some it has evolved into a formalised neo-pagan religion known as Wicca that meets in covens of initiates as regularly and religiously as any church. Much of this is of recent invention based upon dubious historical claims about the survival of ancient underground paganism. Modern Druidism, for example, owes its origins to John Toland in the early eighteenth century, but likes to claim older roots. The Pagan Federation and the Wiccans claim significant increases in their numbers as a result of the Harry Potter books.

Neo-pagan witchcraft, or Wicca, had its inception in the 1940s and 50s, with the writings of Gerald B Gardner, a member of a Southern England traditional coven. Gardner was born on Friday 13th June 1884 in Lancashire. He read *There is No Death* by Florence Marryat, a Spiritualist book, which convinced him both of the survival of the soul after death and of the non-existence of hell. He also read *The Witch Cult in Western Europe* by Margaret Murray in which she credits the idea that medieval witchcraft was a surviving primitive fertility religion.

Gardner's associations included the Legion of Frontiersmen, Freemasonry, the Order of Woodland Chivalry, Theosophy and Spiritualism. In 1920 he revived the "Order of Twelve" as the Crotona Rosicrucian Fellowship. In 1947 he met well-known occultist Aleister Crowley in Hastings and purchased a charter to found a camp of Crowley's magical group. He wrote *High Magick's Aid* in 1954 in which he developed a tradition that was a combination of ritual, ceremonial magick, Crowley's Gnostic Mass, The Key of Solomon, Masonic ritual and French Mediterranean Witchcraft. The Gardnerian Tradition is the basis for most of Modern Wicca.

Wiccans are practitioners of a nature-based religion that follows the seasonal cycles. Their four Greater Sabbats are Samhain, Imbolc, Beltaine and Lammas, and the four Less Sabbats are Yule, Ostara, Litha and Mabon.

A Wiccan/Witch believes that the divine exists within them as well as outside, and feels a direct connection with the god/dess. It is a loosely structured system of beliefs that follows a code of conduct called the Wiccan Rede ('An it harm non, do as thou wilt'). Not all pagans are Wiccans, but all Wiccans are pagans. As in the *Harry Potter* stories, witches are just witches, neither white nor black: evil is a choice, a bad one, not a deity to blame our actions upon. If someone chooses to do evil they will be punished by the laws of karma. The majority of Witches believe in reincarnation, and that karma can follow a person from life to life. Wiccans are neither Christian, Jewish nor Muslim and do not recognise the existence of Satan. They view spells as 'active prayers', a catalyst to create change in one's own life or the life of a loved one. They do not believe in casting harmful spells. Many operate as Solitaries or in small covens, though there are some larger Wiccan churches.

People become Wiccans for many reasons, some of which may be blamed on a church that has failed to offer the gospel in its fullness. Our message has too often been confused and inadequate, our evangelism too urbanised and rationalised. Neglecting spirituality and the Holy Spirit we come across as arrogant and creatively repressed. Associated with the establishment, we were late to address the environment, gender issues and social justice.

Yet a holistic biblical gospel can offer real hope to pagans. In brief, we have an older faith and a better way. The ancient redemptive offering of Abel points to Christ (Hebrews 11:4), granting us peace with the Creator

(Ephesians 2:13–17). The powerful promises of providence replace appeasement with thanksgiving and encourage environmental responsibility. Long live harvest festivals! As a global peace movement we are journeying towards cosmic reconciliation and total wholeness (Colossians 1:16–20), and the Man who holds the cosmos together is greater than the Green Man (Colossians 2:15–17) – and he is the Maker of 'mother earth'.

We also have a true appreciation of the feminine as found in Mother Jerusalem and her emerging earthly expression, the Bride of Christ (Galatians 4:26; Revelation 21:2). This venerable Lady also finds expression as wisdom (Proverbs 8:1–31).

The life, death and resurrection of Christ connect redemption with nature and offer a genuine spiritual rebirth that leads to eternal life and physical resurrection in the renewed cosmos. Jesus breaks the cycle of karma, replacing the circle with an ascending life, death, resurrection wave-form.

Instead of a pentagram we create a spiritual triangle of truth, mercy and humility (Micah 6:8) – a zone of the Spirit operating through the global network of believers united in the Holy Spirit that replaces ley lines and shrines (John 4:21–24). This is manifested wherever local families of believers meet in covenant with each another to minister practical love and grace to one another and to the world around them.

Believers enter the true mystery, which is in you (Colossians 1:26–27). This is the real gnosis that delivers us from the elemental spirits and crucifies the contract of slavery (Colossians 2:14–23), releasing us from the superstitious fear of death brought on by breaking the rules (Hebrews 2:14–15).

We have a Melchizedekian Mediator and High Priest that makes other priests, gurus and masters unnecessary (Hebrews 5:6) and we are initiated into a covenant that atones for all evil and that renders all other sacrifices redundant.

Possessed by the Holy Spirit we are graced and empowered and granted gifts of the Spirit that make occult tools unnecessary. Prayer without props enables us in the Spirit to make a real difference and in meditation to connect at the deepest level with the divine. For we inhabit a genuinely spiritual world of God, angels and demons, of passion and feeling, heroic battles, visions and mystic revelations, curse breaking, healing, deliverance, tongue-speaking, prophetic imagination and symbolism rooted in the reality of Christ and the world.

In the light of all this, what are we to make of the witchcraft of *Harry Potter*? That such a series of books should be written should hardly come as a surprise given the culture in which we find ourselves. How then shall we categorise it?

Recalling our literary analysis earlier in this chapter, it falls mainly into the twin categories of the comic stereotype and of the political manipulation of power. There is nothing very profound about the parodies of popular representations of witchy activities with the misfiring spells and magic sweets, nor even the surreal notions of wizard banks full of gold guarded by goblins (perhaps a version of the gnomes of Zurich). Pouring scorn on such notions of magic is a very effective way of dismissing it to make way for something stronger.

For this is not simply a comic tale serving to debunk popular witchcraft, or even to assuage our fears of such superstitions. The fun side is of a continuum with the more serious side. The teachers at Hogwarts can do real magic; their spells are powerful and they work. It is to be expected that their students will graduate to the same or higher levels. The adult witches can also use their magic on the Muggles, the non-witches that make up ordinary society. That is to say nothing of those who are on the Dark side and, although a moral distinction is drawn between good and bad wizardry, it is not always well drawn. There is no question but that the good guys need to become proficient at the same sorts of magic used by the bad guys. In this respect at least, *Harry Potter* is about as far removed from Narnia as it is possible to be.

Harry Potter presents us with an uneasy spectrum of occult and magic practice that ranges from the frivolous to the truly evil and macabre. It raises the question about where the line is to be drawn. Although some of the characters can be clearly identified as going over to the Dark side, it is assumed that all the rest are by default on the side of light, yet there is no authority for the light side to exist, no reason why it should be so. Even the wizard laws imposed by that parody of Whitehall, the Ministry of Magic, have no basis or appeal to any higher authority.

While the author has made it clear that she has no intention of seducing any one into black magic, given this absence of justification for the light side there is no compelling reason to stop anyone who starts on the occult slope from sliding further than they planned. Children are highly susceptible; they are also prone to their own terrors and nightmares. By putting a smiling face on some aspects of witchcraft, it is too easy for children to experiment, not knowing that in the real world ritual games can, for the vulnerable, lead to a good deal of trouble. How far do you plunge your hand into a dark hole before whatever lurks there bites it? And if it does, what price will you have to pay for it to let go?

Morality without a message, and a message without an author, is ultimately unsustainable. Harry Potter, following his own instincts, will break the laws of the Ministry of Magic or the school rules where occasion demands, simply on the grounds of his innate feelings. To be fair to the author, in most cases Harry's impulsive behaviour gets him into difficulty, and the point is made: that kind of autonomy is dangerous. When everyone does what is right in their own eyes it is the end of civilisation and society. Anarchy builds no roads, only barricades.

Children today are the offspring of parents steeped in situation ethics. Those parents believed that all you needed was love, yet they interpreted love to mean pleasure, notably sexual pleasure, while pretending that it was something virtuous. Today's kids have no such pretensions; the message now is 'all I need is what I want'. If Harry Potter can break the rules, so can I.

The proponents of the so-called Age of Aquarius want to tell us that this is no longer a problem. In their cuckoo world there is no conflict; all is one. Children, and for that matter adults, are innately good. Simply respond to the inner light and conjoin with the Force and all will be well. The only sin is not being yourself; the only demons are those created by the unenlightened.

Would that it were that simple. Take away any ultimate authority for good and evil and our actions boil down to the manipulation of events and people for our own self-interest. Whoever has the best technology wins. As John Andrew Murray has written, contrasting J K Rowling with C S Lewis: 'Rowling's work invites children to a world where witchcraft is 'neutral' and where authority is determined solely by one's might or cleverness. Lewis invites them to a world where God's authority is not only recognised, but celebrated – a world that resounds with his goodness and care.'[1]

Harry Potter's world, though by no means necessarily that of the author, reflects a mentality that, because it has rejected God's authority in favour of political expediency, has given us such horrors as nuclear weapons and chemical and bacteriological warfare, not to mention the obscenity of ethnic cleansing and the poverty brought about by exploitative multinationalism. If you can't draw the line spiritually, you can't draw the line at all, and we are left at the mercy of the power freaks in the playground.

The Bible, by contrast, defines an unmistakable moral line with reference to God himself. There is a kingdom of darkness and there is an overarching kingdom of God's own Son. Much as we may liken our lives to a spiritual journey, there remains a definite point where we cross the immutable line from one kingdom to the other. Christians commonly call this conversion. That line is not fixed by our innate feelings or by some other arbitrary authority. It originates from the living God himself, from none less than the Righteous Judge of all the earth.

The world of *Harry Potter* is devoid of this transcendence; there is nothing for which to aspire, no numinous awe in the presence of goodness, no supreme Other to be sought after or worshipped, no Person to love. Thus, the witchcraft consists of little more than materialistic and psychological manipulation, while failing to reflect reality. In denying the truly spiritual it presents a false world-view, and to this we must now turn.

---

[1] John Andrew Murray, *Faith and Family*, www.familylifecentre.net

6
Worlds Apart

At one time we believed that the Earth was the centre of the universe and the sun and the planets orbited around it while also performing mini-orbits of their own. This complicated and quite wrong view of the solar system was developed by the humanist, Claudius Ptolemy, from ideas proposed by Pythagoras. People believed it for twelve hundred years, until around AD1500 when a Christian, Nicolaus Copernicus, proved that the planets, including Earth, orbit the sun. This major change of model, or paradigm shift, has had a profound effect on Western culture. Today, secular man is lost in space. No longer the centre of everything, he now wonders if he is anything at all. One simple realisation has altered radically the way we see the whole of reality. We have changed our world-view.

Our world-view is the grid through which we interpret our experiences; it is a set of ideas and assumptions that helps us make sense of life. Changing one or more of these assumptions is akin to receiving sight for the first time. For example, it was once believed by a majority of the Western population that black people were a subhuman species; this being so, there was no reason why they could not be harnessed like animals and put to work. Christian evangelists proved that black slaves responded to the gospel. It was an eye-opener and the implication was unavoidable: black people have human souls, they must be emancipated, and we must ask their forgiveness. That paradigm shift led to the abolition of slavery and to the establishment of the UN Charter and the European Convention on Human Rights. We have a different world-view as a result.

The reason why many Christians are unsure about the *Harry Potter* books is not simply because of the plot, or even the use of magic (though they might think so), but because of their underlying world-view. To make sense of this we need to understand the important changes that are taking place in our society – changes that are leading us towards a world-view that we Christians are called to challenge at its very root.

First, the scientific world-view is on the wane. This is not the same as saying that science is dying; it is simply that, as a way of interpreting reality, thoughtful people are finding it increasingly inadequate. A logical nothing-but-ism that reduces our existence to patterns of electrochemical impulses, whose random effects grant us the illusion of freedom, just doesn't do justice to our humanity. Scientists who still teach this have become a bore and their ideas something of a joke. The human spirit cries out for something more and knows it is there. Indeed, our focus on information technology suggests that the universe is information; yet all intelligent information originates from someone. Arguably there is an Informer behind the information. Why did that Informer make us capable of receiving it, and what does it mean?

Secondly, existentialism is ceasing to be! As a reaction to scientific determinism it proved inadequate. 'Now' experiences to authenticate our being have not produced a warm caring society of spiritually sensitive people. Instead, it has hardened into individualism and consumerism and its rock gurus are now just plain rich. Our craving for instant fulfilment has made us the slaves of a push-button technology that grants us sensation without meaning and cost without value. The child of the science against which we rebelled has become our master.

Third, cultural Christianity is a spent force. There are still plenty of old world Christians around, but either they have retreated into the ghetto or they have so imbibed the surrounding culture that they no longer have anything distinctive to offer. Introverted and apologetic, and having no viable apologetic, such Christianity no longer informs the public debate. All that remains is a sort of pragmatic morality – common sense without Christ – that keeps society functioning but which requires more and more legislation and state spying to make it work. Behaviour is no longer constrained by grace but by CCTV cameras.

Old world cultural churches will continue to exist as a monument to the past, much as Guy Fawkes Night or the Last Night of the Proms. TV evangelists can be assured of a wealthy livelihood and middle-class respectability will ensure suburban congregations, but they are irrelevant to the real world – mere consumers of popular culture trailing pathetically in the wake of the world's agenda and offering a belated Christian version to a world that has already made up its mind.

The passing of these three great world-views is what gives us the post-modern world. Although the tides will continue for some time to wash around the sinking islands of the past, a new island is arising from the waters of human history. It is called neo-paganism.

Neo-paganism is a belief in spirituality rather than religion, and in technique rather than relationship. The neo-pagan isn't necessarily a dark demon worshipper and, if he does offer ritual sacrifices in the accepted sense of the term, it is more likely to be as a means of influencing energies rather than of pleasing the gods. Indeed, his spirituality has little to do with a transcendent God or gods. What he will acknowledge is that life is full of mystery and that the sum of all the life energies creates something greater than the whole. Thus he will reverence the earth and honour the connection between *mater*ial and *Mater*, or Mother; he will treat nature as female and, in a non-personal sense, as God.

Our neo-pagan will embark on a journey to discover the spirituality within, but how he does so will depend upon his temperament. He may perceive it as artistic sensibility, or ecological awareness, or the power of positive visualisation, or sexual vitality, or mystic union, or influence over others. Whatever the nature of the quest he will be eager to discover techniques to assist him in making it. These might range from pilgrimages to ancient sites of spirituality to creating a feng shui business environment. Amulets, meditation crystals, statuettes, sexual fetishes, essential oils – the whole array might be used to turn the cosmic force to his advantage. Such a man may advance with the help of a guru and may learn secret mantras, or spells. He will network with others of like mind and may go on to develop a cosmic or mystical connection that enables him to affect the psychological and physical condition of others. If he travels far enough he may aspire to become the Materialist-Magician that C S Lewis anticipated in *The Screwtape Letters*.

In this emerging world-view the concepts of right and wrong take on a different meaning from those of the past, for the scientist sees right and wrong in terms of the provability of a theory, the existentialist as the commitment or otherwise to a leap in the dark, and the Christian in terms of obedience or disobedience to the law of God's love. The scientist puts things right by revising his logic, the existentialist by taking courage, and the Christian by repentance and renewal. The neo-pagan is pragmatic. Did the technique work to further the cause of spiritual enlightenment? Did we network enough energy to produce good magic?

All this brings us to look at the world-view expressed in *Harry Potter*. To be fair to the author, this may or may not reflect her own view – these books are, after all, works of fiction – but they do reflect the trend in our post-Cold War, post-Christian, post-modern society. An important part of their appeal may lie in the measure to which they also reinforce the move towards neo-paganism. This is where, arguably, comparisons with C S Lewis and J R R Tolkien fail. Those authors wrote from a very different world-view. They also addressed a culture that still held to a Christian consensus and that accepted biblical moral and spiritual boundaries. The world today is much altered, as witness how Gandalf in *The Lord of the Rings* could be hijacked by New Agers. Apart from suggestive hints that may point to a deeper intention of the author, the God of the Bible does not fit and cannot fit into the world of *Harry Potter*.

Typical of neo-paganism, Harry Potter makes his redemptive choices unaided by any higher Being. There is no inspiration from above, no Spirit of God at work. Indeed, his is a spiritless world, one that is coloured by the Western value of reason and technology, where manipulation can be taught like a school subject – a sort of non-occultic shamanism where the moral choices have to do only with the end to which the shaman puts his power but not with the techniques themselves. This is spiritually dangerous since in attempting to manipulate what we think is no more than a force, we may fall foul of the purposes of both God and the devil.

In our humanistic arrogance we like to think we can control good and evil – a temptation as old as Eden – but in reality we can't. We need the help of God himself, and if we do not recognise that fact we may just find ourselves at the beck and call of the greatest power freak of all time. Let us make no mistake, however much we like to deny it, evil has an intelligent spirit behind it, one we call Satan. That is why Jesus taught us to pray, 'Lead us not into temptation, but deliver us from the evil one' (Matthew 6:13).

Here are some pertinent words for those who want to dabble in the realm of the spirits:

> There are two equal and opposite errors into which our race can fall about the devils. One is to disbelieve in their existence. The other is to believe, and to feel an excessive and unhealthy interest in them. They themselves (the demons) are equally pleased with both errors and hail a materialist or a magician with the same delight.[1]

The world of *Harry Potter*, though a tale about good and evil, gives no room to a belief in the existence of either God or the devil. Good and evil are simply a matter of choice rather than owing anything to either divine or satanic inspiration. Even the prophecy brought by Sybil Trelawney, the divination teacher, that provides the engine for the story, comes down to a matter of whether you choose to believe it or not. There is no supernatural origin to it, and though there are consequences for society, they are purely

---

[1] C S Lewis, *The Screwtape Letters*, HarperCollins 1942.

humanistic. Although, incongruously, references to God appear as occasional expletives, nobody seeks as such to please or displease him.

> Harry Potter lives in a world free of any religion or spirituality of any kind. He lives surrounded by ghosts but has no one to pray to, even if he were so inclined, which he isn't. Rowling has more in common with celebrity atheists like Christopher Hitchens than she has with Tolkien and Lewis.
>
> What does Harry have instead of God? Rowling's answer, at once glib and profound, is that Harry's power comes from love. This charming notion represents a cultural sea change. In the new millennium, magic comes not from God or nature or anything grander or more mystical than a mere human emotion. In choosing Rowling as the reigning dreamer of our era, we have chosen a writer who dreams of a secular, bureaucratized, all-too-human sorcery, in which psychology and technology have superseded the sacred.[2]

This is overstating it and is excessively cynical. Nevertheless, the world-view that Rowling presents is one that is commonly held by the intellectual establishment, often propagated under the guise of political correctness. Its proponents like to claim that it is objective, 'scientific' and reasonable, but it is nothing of the sort. To rule God – or the devil for that matter – out of the equation takes an *a priori* leap of faith. Secularism, for all its denials, is a religious belief system and in the West arguably no more than the mildewed remains of a spent nineteenth-century liberal Christianity.

Harry Potter's world, while outwardly set in the context of Greco-Roman medieval paganism, is modern. It is impor-

---

[2] Lev Grossman, 'Who Dies in Harry Potter? God', *Time* magazine, Thursday 12 July 2007.

tant to understand this both in terms of the wizarding society and the spells that they perform, and that is why to suggest that Rowling is seducing children into the occult is so misleading. A much more powerful argument would be to suggest that, if anything, she is leading them into a humanistic self-reliance on their own choices, exercise of will, and technological ability – in short, a life that has neither recognition of God nor his grace.

Magic in Harry Potter really isn't magical or transformative. The wizards and witches use it as no more than a form of technology, paralleling in many instances our own world. So Molly Weasley can conjure up automatic potato peeling, while we Muggles (of endless fascination to her husband Arthur) use potato-peeling machines at the touch of a button. Wizards zap people with spells fired from wands; we use guns, rockets, lasers and tasers. Travelling across a city by floo chimneys may be a parodied parallel of the London Underground system. The witches heal by means of potions and spells; we use antibiotics, antidotes and skilled surgery to achieve the same results. The exercise of a spell, like our own technology, depends on intention, will and words, not on prayer, offerings and obedience to supernatural powers or personalities.

Arguably the problem with *Harry Potter* is not that it is too 'into spirits' but that it is not spiritual enough. There is a ceiling that is never passed through; it is at most psychological and political warfare but never spiritual warfare. The best we can draw are some behavioural lessons, and while wishing to commend these and to agree that we should blame neither God nor the devil for our own follies, that is the limit of the journey.

Some disagree with this view and have gone so far as to suggest that Jo Rowling is writing for a post-Christian age a very sophisticated Christian allegory, replete with the code language and mysticism of medieval alchemy and its quest for eternal life – a Christian morality play, no less.

In this view, Rowling is mounting a broadside attack on the secular-materialist world, subverting its technology with a wholly other way of doing life that draws on non-material sources. Her world is deliberately romantic, emotive and relational, and one that is morally superior because love rather than expediency lies at its heart. This world has to be seen 'diagonally'. We are invited to consider beauty, truth and virtue. Indeed, in Diagon Alley the numbers are all primes or the product of primes, pointing us to irreducible eternal qualities, rather than the quantities that obsess the modernist world. Her magic then is a counter-spell to the magic of modernity. As C S Lewis expressed it,

> Do you think I am trying to weave a spell? Perhaps I am; but remember your fairy tales. Spells are used for breaking enchantments as well as for inducing them. And you and I have need of the strongest spells that can be found to wake us from the evil enchantment of worldliness which has been laid upon us for nearly a hundred years.[3]

This is a world that recognises a genuine war between the fascist forces of secularism and those of true humanity – spiritual warfare, no less. This war is, moreover, fought with words and with books. Tom Riddle's diary, smuggled into Ginny Weasley's Transfiguration textbook by Lucius Malfoy, becomes the means of seducing the innocent Ginny into opening the Chamber of Secrets and loosing the Basilisk. It could be a potent allegory for the dangers hiding

---

[3] C S Lewis, *The Weight of Glory*, originally preached as a sermon in the Church of St Mary the Virgin, Oxford, 8 June 1942.

in children's textbooks. By destroying the sentiments and emotions that undergird the virtues of sacrificial love, courage and loyalty, our educationalists have created in children's minds a godlessness and a ruthless self-centredness that corrupts utterly.

John Granger has developed this thesis, suggesting that the whole tale is a Christian redemptive myth, as opposed to being merely the metaphorical Hero's journey.

> Ms. Rowling writes the powerful, spiritual answer in story form . . . in the only language a post Christian culture can understand: she writes in the symbols and doctrines of the Christian faith. Harry Potter fans enjoy a resurrection experience in every book and are awash in word pictures and images of Christ and souls in pursuit of perfection in Him. Without this specific meaning, Rowling could not have achieved her unprecedented popularity in a culture that only knows of God in these forms.[4]

There is much that is attractive in this view. Whether or not Jo Rowling intended it is another matter. Authors can write in a manner that allows interpretations that were not part of their conscious intents but are nonetheless valid. However, as a thesis it raises considerable questions.

The major one is communicability. Whether we like it or not, find it unsophisticated or otherwise, the Christian message is an open secret to be presented to all people in an understandable form. The coded allegory theory turns this plain message of 'Jesus Christ and him crucified' into a gnostic mystery accessible only to the select élite who posses the mystic keys. In the case of *Harry Potter* this would

---

[4] John Granger, 'The Christian Meaning of *The Chamber of Secrets*', http://www.george-macdonald.com/harry_potter_granger.htm

require at the least a knowledge of Latin, Greek, medieval alchemy and arcane symbolism. This knowledge Rowling doubtless possesses, but it is rare. Even should it become a pastime like 'find the hidden message in Harry Potter' it is hardly likely to catch on, requiring as it would a book of codes, a Bible, a gospel analysis and a dictionary. Most people will content themselves with a crossword puzzle or Sudoku. If this is the intention of the author then it is brilliant, but ill-conceived. It may be objected, of course, that the apostle Paul uses proto-gnostic language in Colossians to help his readers make sense of their faith, coming as they did from a culture steeped in mystery religion. Yet, Paul does not shrink from making it crystal clear that the gospel focuses on Christ and the cross. We need redemption, not just enlightenment.

A further problem arises if we do, as John Granger suggests,[5] treat this as a Christian allegory. The two best-known allegories in Christian history are *The Shepherd of Hermas* and *Pilgrim's Progress*. In both these books the author's intention is plain; everything fits the underlying message. When Christian arrives in Vanity Fair or meets Mr Worldly Wise, for example, we are left with no doubt as to the meaning; the metaphors are vivid and imaginative and patently clear. There is nothing like this in the Harry Potter tales.

As a medium, allegory is limited; the plot has to fit the message. Rowling has stated that she doesn't like allegory; nor did C S Lewis and J R R Tolkien. (People sometimes mistake *The Lion, the Witch and the Wardrobe* for allegory, but it isn't. C S Lewis preferred to use the term 'applicability').

---

[5] John Granger, *Looking for God in Harry Potter*, SaltRiver (Tyndale House) 2004.

In other words, his stories may be seen as extended metaphors, that as with all writers come from the author's own world-view, but they stand as simply good stories in their own right.

Rowling may be a declared Christian, but that term is a very wide one embracing everything from right-wing American fundamentalists (which Rowling evidently is not) through intelligent biblical evangelicals to dour Unitarians and excruciatingly PC liberals. Wherever she places herself on the spectrum, it hardly obliges her to stick crosses and doves on the product of her labours or to intend unicorns as Christ figures, the phoenix as the resurrection or the Holy Spirit, Dumbledore as God the Father and Ginny Weasley as the Virgin Mary (actually Ginny is not short for Virginia, but Ginevra) . . . or whatever.

Far better is it to see the Harry Potter series as the Hero's Journey, a mythic redemptive tale like *Star Wars*, *Lord of the Rings* and so forth. As such, there may be many redemptive analogies that we can draw on, some intended by the author, and some inevitable because of the format she has used. By all means let us note the importance of Harry forgiving his enemies, of the way that he is matured through his trials in order to lay down his life for his friends, of the power of love, and much more besides. We may argue, too, that by derivation the mythic structure lends itself to some broadly Christian applications; but let's not take it further than it warrants.

7

Deathly Horrors

It is very much apparent that the world of Harry Potter is not a particularly happy place. The obnoxious Dursley family is humourless enough, but even when Harry escapes into the world of Hogwarts it is far from being a land of fun and games. Harry quickly discovers that his parents were murdered by a vicious psychopath and in many respects this sets the tone for the bleak and brooding atmosphere that pervades the books. Anne McCain likened it to the 'increasingly dark . . . tangled terrain and psychology of Batman movies'.[1]

Perhaps this is hardly surprising when we realise that death is the central theme of the Harry Potter books. Rowling herself candidly acknowledges this:

> My books are largely about death. They open with the death of Harry's parents. There is Voldemort's obsession with conquering death and his quest for immortality at any price, the goal of anyone with magic. I so understand why Voldemort wants to conquer death. We're all frightened of it.[2]

---

[1] Anne McCain, 'More Clay than Potter', *World on the Web*, 30 October 1999.

[2] *Tatler* magazine, 10 January 2006.

This is very personal for Jo Rowling. In 1991 her mother, Anne Volant Rowling, died prematurely at the age of 45 after a ten-year battle with multiple sclerosis, and this traumatic event has had a profound influence on her own life and writing. Perhaps much of *Harry Potter* is about handling grief and waging war on what the Bible calls 'the last enemy to be destroyed' (1 Corinthians 15:26) – significantly one of the only two biblical quotations appearing in the final book. It is also significant that the name Voldemort, meaning Flight from (or of) Death, comes from the same root verb, *volare*, as the middle name of her mother.

The harsh reality of death makes Rowling unsentimental.

> If you are writing about evil, which I am, and if you are writing about someone who is essentially a psychopath, you have a duty to show the real evil of taking human life.[3]

What this produces is a rather sour and sallow world of subdued colours set in a northern clime where bright sunny weather makes a minority appearance. Hogwarts itself is a place of frowning turrets and darkly forbidding chambers guarded by merciless monsters. It is set adjacent to a dangerous lake and a dark forest inhabited by powerful and unrelenting guardians.

Although the children have some fun, there is little joy. There is a distinctly vicious streak in some of the staff and pupils alike. Quidditch is a gladiatorial game where potentially serious injury is part of the sport; it is not for the fainthearted. Students put spiteful hexes and jinxes on one another. The caretaker would torture boys and girls if he were allowed and the Ministry of Magic's temporary replacement for Dumbledore, Dolores Umbridge, does just

---

[3] *Harry Potter and Me*, (BBC Christmas Special) 28 December 2001.

that to Harry. It is hardly surprising, since this is a world where the state employs its own torturers, the Dementors, who not only guard its prison at Azkaban but systematically destroy the personalities of its wretched inhabitants. The justice system is ruthless but also open to infiltration and corruption, and this is echoed in Hogwarts. Here the rules are stern and supposedly impartial, yet Snape, while appearing just, can manipulate the rules to bring misery into Harry's life.

This is a world of the macabre where odd is normal and horrors await the unwary and terrors haunt our dark places. You would not wish to go there and if you did you could well find yourself fighting for your life – and your sanity. For this is a world where Voldemort can appear as the face on the back of Quirrell's head, where his gigantic serpent, Nagini, can slither out of an old woman's severed neck. Here you will find a graveyard in which a freakish 'baby' is thrown into a heated caldron and a servant amputates his own hand and draws some of Harry's blood, casting both into the simmering cauldron and thus allowing Voldemort to rise from his semi-dead existence into a full-blown manifestation of evil. Pain is a reality; people are tortured mercilessly with the *Cruciatus* curse, screaming their agony to unheeding ears, driven to death or to insanity by their sufferings. Violence abounds, sometimes trivialised by the ease with which magic-wielding medics can mend stuff that in our world would either cripple you for life or would take months if not years to heal. Monstrous spiders, violent giants, sinister Death Eaters, untamable dragons, terrifying Dementors – they are all here and, although Rowling is never gratuitous with her violence, neither does she spare our emotions.

Of course, children love monsters and monstrosities and

Rowling's point is that it is better to face our fears in the safe context of a novel than in real life. However, the impressionable can find that instead of facing fear and overcoming it, with the author's help, fears and images that did not before exist are now implanted into their minds. The same applies to the sombre tone of the books. It may be argued that to read such depressing stuff as escapism will enable children to be happier with their own lot, but it might also trigger a morose and pathological outlook on life in the same way that some rock music has done just that to vulnerable fans.

The lesson for parents seems clear: know your own child and have a say in what they are exposed to and when. It may be a cruel world, but it is not wholly cruel and children are surely entitled to their innocence longer than we currently allow. We should also note that while Harry Potter's life grows bleaker as he grows up, it by no means follows that life must become darker as we approach adulthood. Our children should be encouraged into an optimistic future without calling it unreality.

The major focus of the darkness in *Harry Potter* is Voldemort and his followers, the Death Eaters. This is the truly sinister stuff. Harry's adventures take us unrelentingly into the darkness, into the heart of evil. Voldemort, driven by his desire for immortality, is utterly ruthless. Those who oppose him are tortured and murdered. He almost seems to gain substance by the deaths of others, and he is able to possess those over whom he has power, as with Quirrell in the first volume – and he will stop at nothing to destroy the one person who, even as a baby, had the power to quell him.

Some might think that Voldemort is a metaphor for the devil, but this is a world where, as we noted earlier, neither God nor the devil exists. Great as Voldemort's power is, he is clearly shown to be of human origin, and although his 'binding and loosing' might be seen as a parallel to the millennial binding of Satan in Revelation 20:1–3, it is stretching the point.

Nor does Voldemort make a good metaphor for death. After all, it is death he is trying to avoid. As Rowling reminds us, written on the tombs of Harry's parents, in a Christian graveyard, are the words of 1 Corinthians 15:26, 'The last enemy to be destroyed is death.' In the end, Voldemort will succumb to that enemy himself.

Death in Rowling's work is immensely powerful. 'There is no spell to reawaken the dead,' says Dumbledore after the death of Cedric at the hands of Voldemort. The headmaster does bring some comfort, but it is small: 'There is nothing to be feared from a body, Harry, any more than there is anything to be feared from the darkness. It is the unknown we fear when we look upon death and darkness, nothing more.' Fair enough as far as it goes, but it is a view far removed from the Christian hope of entering Christ's presence, let alone anticipating the resurrection of the body at the return of Christ.

Consistent with this, the funeral of Dumbledore is stoic. All we can do is keep on fighting to keep evil at bay, but the battle will never cease. During the funeral we are distanced from the oration and taken away into Harry's own grieving thoughts. There is no graveside promise of resurrection for Dumbledore, 'in sure and certain hope of eternal life' such as you would expect at a Christian funeral. As with the death of Sirius, we are left with tragedy and no more than voices beyond the veil.

This was very much the world of old paganism in which the ancient Greco-Roman myths were framed, and in which redemption was hard to come by. Life was short-lived and fearful; surrounded by nameless dreads, knowing not where they came from nor whence they would go, people turned to the occult adepts whose magic arts appeared to offer some solace against the vagaries of Fate. It was small comfort; paganism offers a bleak and cynical world compared to the light and joy of the government of heaven. For all its honourable desires to find spiritual meaning, it has lost the way to the tree of life, for it has lost Christ in a confusion of lesser deities, rituals and rubrics. Its old religion is not old enough, nor powerful enough, for, 'In the beginning was the Spell, and the Spell was with God, and the Spell was God . . . and the Spell became human and lived among us, full of grace and truth' (*see* John 1:1,14). The ultimate effectual word – that is what a spell claims to be – is a Person, the Logos, the Son of God who on the cross, in C S Lewis' words, performed a 'deeper magic' that dis-spells evil and opens the path of transformational enlightenment through spiritual union with himself.[4]

However, deliverance was to come to the pagan world. One day an army of ordinary people, refusing to carry weapons yet capable of performing miracles, began to tell a new story wherever they travelled. It wasn't the tale of an awe-inducing wizard, nor of a misfit spear-wielding mercenary, nor of a super-zapping sky warrior, all of whom might be as terrifying as the enemies that they had come to vanquish. Instead, it was the simple story of the day when God the Creator took the form of a baby, lived our life and died our death and, as sure as the turn of the season, rose again

---

[4] Those who object to my use of Spell to translate Logos might prefer Empowered Seminal Reason, but I am trying to reach 21st-century pagans not 1st-century pagans. Either way 'Word', in our current use of the term, is an inadequate translation.

to give life to the world. It was the tale of innocent blood shed for the sins of the guilty, of the promise of life after death, of adoption into the love and grace of God. Such a message was already written in the natural order and hinted at in the myths of the past. It could transform the culture without abolishing it, so that the best would be purified and the worst removed. Needing no violence, it was embraced by Jews, Greeks, Romans, Persians and Celts alike, because in the truest sense it was a better story.

Rowling's portrayal of the remorselessness of death is realistic concerning our feelings of finality and loss. We should never minimise our grief with trite platitudes, nor trivialise the most unnatural and universal thing that ever happens to humans. As Colin Murray Parkes put it, 'Grief is the price we pay for love,'[5] and we should not skimp on the payment. Nor should we forget that death itself is grievous. Death came into the world through sin, and the sin of Adam tainted the whole human race with its curse. Worse, it is followed by judgement: 'man is destined to die once, and after that to face judgment' (Hebrews 9:27).

The Bible does not teach universalism, the notion that God's love is so great or the death of Christ so effectual that everyone gets to heaven irrespective of their beliefs or behaviour. Such a view would make nonsense of our profoundest beliefs about justice. Unwelcome as the thought is, there is a heaven and a hell and people go to one or the other depending on their relationship with Christ and the behaviour that flows from that. That has to be just. After all, if someone says that they have no time for God, no liking for his followers, no interest in serving Jesus, why would

---

[5] Colin Murray Parkes, *Bereavement*, Tavistock Publications 1972; Penguin Books 1998.

they ever complain if they found themselves excluded from the presence of God and his people in the afterlife? If you reject the lifebelt thrown to you, don't be surprised if you are swept away in the flood.

Let's be clear: God is no sadist. He does not wish any to perish (2 Peter 3:9), but nor can he cease to be just, any more than the laws of the universe can be arbitrarily suspended because he feels sorry for the man who decides he can fly without wings despite all warnings to the contrary.

Nor do demons torture people in hell. It is the place of their punishment, not of their pleasure. We should not imagine hell as a great orgy either. Hell is outer darkness – it speaks of endless isolation and loneliness. Mocking the imagery will not help – metaphors represent a reality beyond experience and comprehension, but reality it is.

The good news, of course, is that hell is totally avoidable and a place in heaven can be guaranteed, and that is the message of the gospel. So the church, while being honest about hell, should spend the major part of its energies inviting people to heaven. 'Everyone who calls on the name of the Lord will be saved' (Romans 10:13). Very simply, by putting faith in the death of Christ for our sin and becoming one of his devoted followers, we receive the assurance of eternal life. Why should anyone have a problem with that? It is all we have to do, and if we refuse because of hardness of heart, rebellion, self-centredness, hatred of Christians or the church, we have only ourselves to blame – and we forfeit any right to criticise God for his way of ordering the universe.

At the heart of the Christian message is hope. Christ is risen. Someone has come back from the dead. Not only does it demonstrate the reality of life after death (as opposed to all sorts of dubious near-death experiences) but it reveals for those who put their faith in him the reality of heaven, a place of fellowship with God and his people, of endless delight in the garden of God.

There is more. Christ is coming back, and when he does this world as we know it will end and be remade as a new cosmos in which righteousness dwells. Followers of Christ will be resurrected to gain supra-physical bodies. We will not be drifting around eternity in night shirts plucking harps, but will enjoy the endless creative wonder of an entire universe untainted by evil or death. The last enemy will have been destroyed for good. Thank God for that!

8

The Politics of Power

It is perfectly possible to have morality without God. One simply argues for moral relativism, taking the line that the human race through its great ethical teachers has evolved a set of behavioural norms for the genetic survival of the community. 'Do unto others. . .'; 'love your neighbour as yourself' give us the basis for a kind of justice that is best expressed in egalitarianism – fair play for all, equal rights, toleration of minorities, pluralism and so forth. So, Jesus is acceptable and respected as a moral teacher, but not as Lord and Saviour. The latter role is distinctly religious and therefore unacceptable. You can aspire to be good; you must surrender to be saved!

Moral relativism and situation ethics can be challenged at any number of levels, and ever since the Enlightenment philosophers and political theorists have had to struggle to save the notion from inevitable scepticism. The reasons are simple: if there is no Absolute Being then there is no compelling basis for justice, obedience or sacrifice. Law becomes defined by the whims of those in power and the easily manipulated voters. Further, the evolutionary notion of the survival of the fittest runs counter to loving your neighbour.

My rights come to dominate to the point where I want to do as I like, and never mind the rest. Without God there can be no aspiration, no divine vision, nothing to lift us from the slough of selfishness.

Nobody saw this more clearly, and with such devastating consequences, than Friedrich Nietzsche. Despairing of good and evil, he saw only power. We must lose all sentiment, all weakness, all notions of love. Power must conquer and it must do so without remorse.

The political implications of Nietzsche are written in blood across the twentieth century, in the rise of both communism and fascism, where the state came to assume absolute power. Today it is seen in the militarism of the West and in the steady erosion of freedom, personal choice, individual responsibility, and the right to speak. This is becoming characteristic of our educational, broadcasting and political institutions, governed as they are by proponents of an increasingly fascist political correctness.

All this Rowling takes on, from Quirrell's recitation of Nietzsche's ideology in the first book, through to Voldemort's obtaining the all-powerful Elder Wand in the last. The lines are clearly drawn: inhuman power or sacrificial love – and only one can win.

This is not so easy as it seems. The wizarding community is élite and aristocratic. Its members have extraordinary powers. They are a secret society of arcane Gnostics with their own school, bank and shops accessed by secret passwords and spells; a higher order of beings possessed of occult knowledge that grants them great advantages over lesser mortals. The witch children all receive a private education, and even though the poor like the Weasleys struggle financially, they are a world removed from the average Muggle comprehensive. Harrry Potter, though he is devoid of greed, is the heir to a fortune that he can take for granted, and he gets the best of everything in the bargain.

The non-wizards are the Muggles (mugs all), portrayed in the case of the revolting Dursleys with some crude cultural stereotyping. The Dursleys are selfish petty bourgeoisie, clueless irritants with 'a medieval attitude towards magic'. Yet, while their behaviour is inexcusable, their birth is not. Half of Britain is made up of ordinary middle-class people who through no choice of their own are holding down regular, if boring, jobs and living in ordinary suburban houses.

True, in the last book Dudley does barely manage some gratitude to Harry as they depart for the last time from one another's lives, but he cannot become a wizard, even if he wished to, and nor can his parents. The best they could do is to change their attitude towards wizards – something they fail to do even at this last farewell.

The rules of birth determine whether you are a Muggle or a wizard; you cannot change and, if magic is a metaphor for spiritual values, there is no hope for you to participate in that higher life. You were born wrong. It all smacks of a Hindu caste system or an apartheid South Africa. How different from Jesus who would be known as the Friend of Muggles, and would open the spiritual world to them whatever their birth. You can be born again!

Yet, having created this world Rowling is crystal clear about the responsibilities of the wizarding community towards Muggles, and her lines of right and wrong are drawn with uncompromising clarity. Again we are reminded of Nazi Germany. Voldemort and his Death Eaters aspire to rid the world of Mudbloods, those with non-wizard parents, reminiscent of the persecution of the Jews and gypsies. (Like Adolf Hitler, who hardly resembled the blond-haired, blue-eyed Aryans he so much admired, Voldemort is himself a Half-blood who seeks eternal life through power to redeem his ancestry. Hitler's 'eternal life' was to be the Third Reich.) Pure-bloods must rule, not only within their own community, but over the Muggles as well. Indeed, Muggles are fair game for capricious murder and torture. Other races are treated with equal disdain, like bonded house elves and goblins (though the latter are hardly saints).

In stark contrast to this is Arthur Weasley's unabashed love of Muggles and his political attempts to protect them by means of the Muggle Protection Act. There is also Hermione Granger's well-meant campaign to liberate house elves from their class-conditioned servitude.

Above all, Dumbledore, McGonagall and others, especially of the noble House of Gryffindor, are firmly set against fascism. Dumbledore's past is mixed and full of regrets for having once himself believed that wizards should rule the Muggles 'for the greater good'. The three Deathly Hallows had come into his possession – the Invisibility Cloak, the Resurrection Stone, and the deadly Elder Wand. Yet, tempted as he was, Dumbledore had seen the consequences of untrammelled power in Grindelwald, the man he had once admired. Refusing power himself, Dumbledore makes it his life mission to oppose racism and fascism.

His opportunity arrives with the appearance of Harry Potter, a baby able to defeat the irresistible curse, *Avada Kedavra*, because of the greater power of his mother's sacrificial love. Carefully nurtured by Dumbledore, Harry is finally ready to fulfil his destiny: he must willingly and without resistance lay down his life for his friends. Yet Harry's choice comes earlier when he too is tempted to seek the Elder Wand. Choosing to hunt down the horcruxes rather than the hallows determines that Harry will follow the higher calling and so save his race and the Muggle world from intolerable tyranny. It is the choice that faced Frodo Baggins at the Cracks of Doom, and like him Harry has his own 'resurrection' and returns to liberate his people. This is consistent with the Greco-Roman Hero's journey, and to the extent that this reflects the divine drama of the Hebrew-Christian revelation, lends itself as a partial metaphor for Christ's redemptive act.

What Rowling sees so clearly is that the threat of Voldemort's terror forces bad government into ever more repressive measures, as when the Ministry of Magic appoints the sweetly evil Dolores Umbridge as temporary head of Hogwarts. Devoid of any real humanity, she is representative of those elements that believe only endless restrictive legislation can produce a safe society. Control and conformity becomes everything; individualism must be quelled – even if it requires regrettable measures like torturing Harry Potter for his own good, or employing the nightmare Dementors and draconian courts to lock away so-called undesirables and nonconformists. It is a pertinent warning to the West as it begins again to justify torture in the name of the 'war on terror', and in this Rowling stands with George Orwell's prophetic *1984* and his portrayal of Big Brother (as far removed from the TV trash as is imaginable and much more true to life). Rowling will allow no moral justification for state torture and murder, or the incarceration of protesters. These are unequivocal evils and those who participate or condone such practices are damned.

Not only do such measures lack the power to defeat evil, they are in themselves a surrender to evil. There is only one answer: a subversive movement based upon different values. The Order of the Phoenix is just that for adults, and for Harry Potter and his close friends. But students must do the same, and Harry initiates the formation of the Defence Association ('Dumbledore's Army') in the Room of Requirement. Students must rise up and rebel not only against Voldemort but against a fatally flawed intrusive and repressive government that will in any event topple like a house of cards. The resistance will go underground, have to suffer media lies and misleading government propaganda, and finally confront the enemy with a decisive self-sacrificing heroism. In so doing, it will redeem society from the thrall of the enemy, and no other way will do because evil cannot defeat evil, darkness cannot put out darkness. *Harry Potter* is a heart cry for someone please to listen to this!

Only love can overcome evil; only light extinguishes darkness. It is the message of Christ and it is exemplified in his own laying down of his life, not only for his friends, but also for his enemies. This is C S Lewis' 'deeper magic'. The apostle Paul put it this way: 'I will destroy the wisdom of the wise; the intelligence of the intelligent I will frustrate . . . For the foolishness of God is wiser than man's wisdom, and the weakness of God is stronger than man's strength . . . God chose the foolish things of the world to shame the wise; God chose the weak things of the world to shame the strong' (1 Corinthians 1:19, 25, 27). If you wish to glorify, then glorify the God who is Love.

Paul's context was a world under the dictatorial control of a fascist government, the Roman Empire, whose very symbol of judicial authority was the *fasces*, a bundle of wands with an axe in the centre. As in *Harry Potter*, it makes all the more potent the decision to reject the kingdom of force and to embrace the way of sacrificial love. That same choice confronts the church today. The weapons of our warfare are not carnal; we too are forbidden to use the *Cruciatus* curse (the word reminds us of crucifixion as used to enforce the rule of Rome). Instead, we are to love our enemies; we 'defeat' them by our good works, by the light of our lives and our actions.

We all must ask ourselves: what kind of world do we want? Will we choose the tyranny and violence of a repressive state and embrace its ruthless, inhuman values; or will we opt for the way of Christ that alone offers us true humanity and personal freedom? Many despair of the latter, feeling that the church has sold out to the spirit of the age. But there is hope, and it is time for us to consider a better story.

9
A Better Story

Old world cultural Christianity may be finished in the West, but the faith itself is as vibrant as ever. With roots older than time, it remains as fresh as an early summer's dawn and is on the brink of a significant resurgence. What a stark and cheerful contrast it makes to the bleak world of paganism, where winter never quite ends and spring is for ever uncertain!

Rowling paints the pagan scene well. Christmas at Hogwarts celebrates light without the Light, it is a feast without the Guest, gifts are given but the Gift is not received, devoid of angels it is empty of praise, for no Saviour is born, no Baby fills the crib. We must live another year in the chill shadow of Voldemort.

Yet, in contrasting reality, 'to us a child is born, to us a son is given, and the government will be on his shoulders. And he will be called Wonderful Counsellor, Mighty God, Everlasting Father, Prince of Peace' (Isaiah 9:6).

Of all the great religious and secular systems in the world, only the Christian faith provides an adequate base for hope, because only the Christian faith has a doctrine of grace and truth incarnated in Jesus of Nazareth, the Son of God. Only the Christian faith presents us with God revealing himself in terms that we can understand.

For Jesus isn't Superman or ET; he is our kind of man, feeling as we do, limited as we are, yet under the anointing of the Holy Spirit, demonstrating the reality of God's intervention in the pain and confusion of human experience. Who cannot wonder at the words and works of this man, whose eyes could set your heart on fire, whose voice could still the storm and stir the soul, whose strong hands could heal the sick and raise the dead? Should we not follow the Good Shepherd who lays down his life for the sheep? For Jesus dies, the willing Victim for others, tearing down the façade of religion, outfacing the satanic accuser with irrefutable righteousness, satisfying the most exacting demands for justice, and winning cynical hearts with the greatest demonstration of unconditional love ever shown.

Then God raises him from the dead. The Prince of Life arises victorious over the ultimate enemy to bring life and hope to all who believe, and to break the shackles of deceitful night. Striding through the ranks of awed lesser powers, he takes his place by right as Lord of all and receives the nations as his inheritance, whereupon, as Head of the church, he sends forth his Holy Spirit to announce through the lives, words and miracles of his people the forgiveness of sins, reconciliation with the Father, freedom from Satan's grip, and a life of endless transformation lived out in a community of grace.

True, this grace is often subverted by Christians themselves into legalism and into licence, and truth is sometimes reduced to opinion and ecclesiastical convenience, but these are errors. The truth that is Christ is incorruptible and all true seekers will find him.

This gospel comes with a universal appeal that excludes

nobody from the offer of salvation. The voluntary humility of Jesus flies right in the face of proud human hierarchies. Jesus emptied himself of his rightful trinitarian equality with God to become like one of us – and lower – and that is why the gospel bars no one on the grounds of birth, gender, education or economic status. Witches, Mudbloods and Muggles alike can be saved! 'You are all sons of God through faith in Christ Jesus, for all of you who were baptised into Christ have clothed yourselves with Christ. There is neither Jew nor Greek, slave nor free, male nor female, for you are all one in Christ Jesus' (Galatians 3:26–28). Apologies to all modern-day egalitarians, feminists, socialists, but Jesus got there two thousand years before you, and he did so without recourse to bitterness and violence, nor did he exchange one tyranny for another.

Not only does the gospel welcome everyone in on an equal footing, but it also gives everyone an equal access to the mystery of the faith: under the instruction of the Holy Spirit it is an open secret for all to explore. Spiritual growth is not a matter of mastering secret esoteric techniques but of developing a loving relationship with the Almighty: We 'grow in the grace and knowledge of our Lord and Saviour Jesus Christ' (2 Peter 3:18).

This means that true followers of Christ do not live by a set of carefully cultivated rules, complete with orders of merit, but by a living relationship with Jesus who truly 'fills full' the law of God. This relationship begins with an inner transformation so powerful that it can only be described as a spiritual rebirth, and it results in a life filled with the dynamic energy of the Holy Spirit that progressively turns obedience to God's will into a living instinct of grace. Instead of treating the Sermon on the Mount as a new set of rules imposed from without, the believer discovers this law of love written on his heart, so that it can be willingly lived out in love for God and love for our neighbours.

As such, the gospel message laid the foundations for true community and historically has provided the greatest incentive to enlightened civilisation, despite all the corruption and resistance of kings and politicians alike. It is to this gospel that we owe our democracies, our universal education, our health services and our social welfare institutions. This Christian God-spell, the truth Myth, by its own intrinsic power broke the cynicism and despair of the pagan world because it addressed the real needs of people with a real solution.

The trouble is, everyone wants what Christians have but without the message that makes it possible in the first place. The world is full of hypocrites! Political systems cannot produce what only grace has the power to do. At best they mimic it. Even less will neo-paganism succeed.

Modern paganism does, of course, recognise the reality of good and evil, but because it misunderstands the cause it cries out for no more than a hero. Heroism was considered by the pagan Greeks to be the greatest of virtues – something Jesus agreed with when he said that 'greater love has no-one than this, that he lay down his life for his friends' (John 15:13) – and Jesus himself is the greatest hero that ever lived. Yet we will have to go much further than *Harry Potter*. He may draw inspiration from his mother's love in his times of greatest need, but he draws no inspiration from God. A mother's love to save her child is instinctive; by contrast, Jesus chose freely and with no other constraint than his love for sinners to lay down his life for us. That's real inspiration!

At the heart of the Christian gospel lies the death and resurrection of Christ. Jesus wasn't just a hero who beat up the devil, or who inspired us to overcome the dark side of our psyches. He made atonement for us. This is the doctrine that modern-day pagans hate. To suggest that we need reconciliation by means of a blood sacrifice offends them because their world is one where everyone is good unless corrupted by others – a half-truth that adds up to a complete error! Like it or not, there is a fundamental and fatal ego bias in all of us that makes us want to be as gods without God. We have eaten from the wrong tree and it has poisoned us to death. That is why it took someone to die on a tree to bring us back to life.

> As for you, you were dead in your transgressions and sins, in which you used to live when you followed the ways of this world and of the ruler of the kingdom of the air, the spirit who is now at work in those who are disobedient. All of us also lived among them at one time, gratifying the cravings of our sinful nature and following its desires and thoughts. Like the rest, we were by nature objects of wrath. But because of his great love for us, God, who is rich in mercy, made us alive with Christ even when we were dead in transgressions – it is by grace you have been saved. And God raised us up with Christ and seated us with him in the heavenly realms in Christ Jesus (Ephesians 2:1–6).

This has to be the most positive psychology in the world, for it truly releases us from the bondage to our past, and it provides us with both the power and the presence of God to live for the future. Winter really does end and summertime begin.

The world of the Christian is one that brings to bear upon the sadnesses and corruptions of life the beautifying and energising grace of the Holy Spirit and the redemptive power of Christ. This is not a world of dark demons but a world of bright fellowship, of gifts granted freely and of grace generously bestowed. It engages us in spiritual warfare, but it does so with the help of a world of angels ministering on behalf of the elect. Sure there are demons and principalities and powers, and sometimes the battle is hard, but the victory is assured through the name of Jesus and the blood of Calvary.

To proclaim this message of grace is the mission calling and the task of the church. We are an apostolic community commissioned and empowered to announce the good news of Jesus Christ to every person on the planet without fear or favour. We have no need whatsoever to be ashamed of this message, for it carries God's power to transform lives and it does so today with ever-increasing effectiveness right across the globe.

The truly missionary church has met paganism and secularism many times in its history and has overcome them every time by refusing to use military power or deceit. Instead, we have told the simple story of Jesus, shown a defenceless love to all people, lived lives of joyful piety, and performed better miracles than the pagans. We have done all this out of profound gratitude to Jesus and with a persistent passion to see his gracious government established in the hearts and lives of men, women and children the world over.

Where does *Harry Potter* fit into all this? In a remarkable manner the last book in the series reveals another subtext that puts J K Rowling firmly *within* the world of Lewis, Tolkien and the Inklings. There is no obvious allegory, no single thread, no spoiling of the pagan mythic structure, but there are unmistakable Christian motifs woven like jewels into the fabric of the tale. These include the words of Jesus, 'Where your treasure is, there will your heart be also' (*see* Matthew 6:21) on the graves of Dumbledore's mother and sister, in a Christian churchyard, and 'The last enemy that shall be destroyed is death' (1 Corinthians 15:26) found on the graves of Harry's parents and drawn from Paul's great exposition of resurrection. Even the reference to the Resurrection Stone draws us to the one faith that proclaims a truly risen Lord and Saviour.

Then there are references to the cross. We might understandably miss the first King's Cross Station as a place of spiritual decision and transition – anyone who has been there will understand why! – but there is little mistaking the one at the climax of *Deathly Hallows*: having laid down his life willingly for the world, Harry finds himself in a heavenly King's Cross where he must choose to return to aid his friends or journey on into eternal life. What is the King's Cross but the cross of Christ the King? What is it but the place where eternal life begins? It is evident that mortal death is not the end; there is a future life beyond the grave and it bears no resemblance to Philip Pullman's dishonest parody, nor to the recycling machine of the pantheists. We have moved beyond the mirror of desire, Erised. This is more than wish fulfilment or a projection of our deepest feelings. Nor are we in the unrested world of ghosts, those echoes and imprints of people who either declined to enter, or were restrained from entering, their future. Dumbledore is there and ready to travel on. Harry may do the same if he so desires.

We should not neglect, either, the cross symbol revealed in the way that Lily Potter defended her son, not clutching him as would be expected of a mother, but by forming an outstretched cruciform body before him and making a fully determined decision to lay down her life for him. Thus when the silver doe, so representative of his mother, guides Harry to the sword of Gryffindor, what he sees first beneath the ice is a silver cross.

There are other clues too. Sirius is Harry's godfather. You can't have one of these without a God! Christmas may be pagan but somehow Christmas carols sneak in, and Christian Christmas is being celebrated in the church even as Harry searches for his parents' graves – so those occasional expletive references of God may not be so incongruous after all.

Supreme is Harry's forsaking of his friends, his love, his life, knowing that he, unarmed and willingly, must die at the hands of Voldemort. In so doing he invokes the Narnian 'deeper magic', undergoes his own near-resurrection experience and finally destroys Voldemort with his own weapon. Let the free world rejoice!

These clues are there for those who want to find them, and we should certainly help our children to see them. More than that, it is time to train a new generation for the unfinished task of spreading the good news to their generation.

10
Train Up a Child

Educating children in wisdom is a fundamental responsibility that we may not shirk. If we don't do it, someone else will attempt it, and unless we are very sure of their credentials and motives, we will be advised to take on the task ourselves.

Wisdom begins with protection. When my mother shielded my eyes from seeing the results of an horrific road accident at the age of four she was quite right. That may sound like common sense, but it is amazing just how many parents allow their children to watch violent and sexually explicit content on the TV channels, and how many permit them unlimited access to the Internet, let alone caring not a bit about what they are reading. This is not only stupid, it is downright irresponsible. As we pointed out earlier in this book, the images embedded in childhood do without doubt influence a child's later life. All parents, teachers and youth workers have a responsibility to exercise a degree of censorship over the material to which the children in their care are exposed, and that must include what goes on in the school classroom.

As cultural gatekeepers we must know when to exercise

caution and when to make an outright ban. Some material will never be appropriate because it is implicitly evil in intent and in content. Other material may depend upon the age and sensibility of the individual child. The fact that something is considered to be entertaining or 'everyone's reading it' is not in itself a sufficient justification for letting children participate.

That said, we should beware of knee-jerk reactions. If we overreact for the wrong reasons, for example, simply because of 'scare words' like 'witch' or 'ghost' in the title, our children are likely to consider us pathetic and out of touch. Once they lose respect for our judgement they will form their own, but without the experience of life that teaches us where the safe boundaries are. Or they may grow up paranoid, fearing to read or watch anything that doesn't have a cross or a holy pigeon on the cover in case they become contaminated. That may produce either reactionary bigots in adult life or those who kick over the traces once they discover the pleasure that has been denied them for so long.

Even if we do feel it right to ban certain materials from our children's cultural intake, let us make sure that they don't feel deprived or even punished. Provide something better instead. A good substitute is always better than a one-sided outright ban. A friend of ours, not approving of Pokemon for his eight-year-old son, asked him to dispose of the cards and explained why. After a few days of indecision, the boy did so. On the basis of the child's own choice, the father bought him a really decent football, much to the boy's delight.

Our task as Christians is to be proactive in the world. Instead of just reacting against everything that we dislike, we are to propagate the better message of the gospel.

Without shame, we should bring its values to bear on every aspect of our lives and the lives of our children. Censorship is not enough; we must teach our children to think and to discern the difference between good and evil, and to make good use of that acquired wisdom in furthering the faith within themselves and among their peers.

This is a learned process. The ability to discern between good and evil comes about by experience: 'Solid food is for the mature, who by constant use have trained themselves to distinguish good from evil' (Hebrews 5:14). We should not expect our children to become wise at one sitting! Nor does it come about by hard study – which may be a relief to some – but by the renewal of minds and bodies yielded to the Lord's service. If we are to train our children in wisdom, we must read and watch much of what they read and watch, and we must ensure that these matters are open season for discussion.

Harry Potter isn't the best starting point for younger children, but with children of, say, eleven-plus it does provide an opportunity to help them reflect morally and spiritually. Before that age there are many better stories that can provide good myth and adventure from a theistic and often Christian world-view. Not that we should be afraid to let our children read books written by non-Christians or books that do not have an explicitly religious theme. Indeed, there is a good argument for keeping religious figures out of fairy tales, so that there will be no doubt in children's minds that these are of a different order from salvation history. Father Christmas is fine as a fanciful story, but Father Christmas meets Jesus or the apostle Peter is confusing. Nor need God be mentioned explicitly; the world-view of the book may allow the character of God to shine through the players in the story.

Even pagan myths can reflect on reality. One of the reasons why the ancient Celts surrendered their beliefs in favour of Christianity was because they found that it provided the fulfilment of so much that their myths and traditions had hoped for. Since we are considering a modern story written after the mythic pattern we can use *Harry Potter* as a means of helping our children gain discernment.

Harry Potter is set in a parallel world that interchanges and interacts with our own. This raises questions about the nature of reality. Is there an invisible world? Can we enter it? The film *The Matrix* portrayed a parallel world in Platonist terms and it had many students and adults thinking about an alternative to materialism. The Bible indicates at least three realms of reality: the visible world, the heavenly places, and the third heaven. We should encourage our children and teens to read the book of Revelation. They will not understand all the symbolism, but the book will open their eyes to a reality beyond the material and intellectual. This is the realm where Christ is seated in glory and where Christians, seated with him, share in his authority. It is also the amphitheatre where the spiritual war is fought. How much are your children aware of this as they study at school and college?

Conflict is a central theme in the *Harry Potter* tales, as it is also in the Bible. The Scriptures affirm that this world is ruled by a good Creator who himself is uncreated. God and the devil are not equal. Satan is but a creature; spiritual, but severely limited in his attributes. Unlike God he cannot be everywhere, know everything, or do just what he wants. For this reason, children should not fear the devil. Instead, they should trust in the Lord and worship him for his goodness. You should take the opportunity to discuss good and evil with your children. It is a major concern. Rowling introduces a lot of death into her books, providing a chance to talk about that most taboo of subjects.

Harry Potter's world is full of taboos and rules. Such a place has little room for the relaxed open-heartedness of grace. Life clearly does have its dangers, but just how defensive should we be? Is there no place left for trust in this cynical world? Christians have always trusted that the Lord's angels will look after them. How relevant is this to your children in today's world?

It would be hard to avoid the connection between severe depression, mental breakdown, and the Dementors as portrayed by J K Rowling. Her coined term is clearly a direct reference to being 'demented' – out of one's mind. Depression, suicide and breakdowns are tragically common among teenagers. Discuss with them why this is so and talk, too, about the reality of demons and of angels. We have a better remedy than the Patronus proposed in the *Harry Potter* story, though it may be indicative. The comforts of Christ's victory, the help of the Holy Spirit, the Strengthener, and the vision of future glory are powerful weapons. Many of us, knowing the assault of evil, have found immense power in the name of Jesus. As for the illegal *Cruciatus* curse, let it point to that most powerful remedy in the deliverance wrought by the crucifixion of Christ.

The excellent virtue of love and loyalty among friends is prominent in *Harry Potter*. It is tested and tried. Sometimes it is revealed to be false, and sometimes what appears to be false turns out to be remarkably true. Our children have to learn discernment when it comes to friendships. They must learn, too, the moral limits of loyalty. One of the follies of our modern media is to portray calf love as an infallible virtue, leading teenagers to rebel against all authority and good sense in its pursuit. Help your children to discern the difference between true love and immature obsession.

The love shown in *Harry Potter* is noble. Love between people is part of God's common grace in the world; we may not like it, but even Hitler loved his mistress, Eva Braun. Truly Christian love is more than that and has its own Greek word *agape*. This is willing self-sacrificing love that extends even to our enemies – a love that Harry extends even to the Malfoy family. Jesus called us to love and to forgive even our enemies. This raises very real issues for our children. What do you do about the school bully? How can you forgive those who maim innocent people?

Harry is interested in the meaning of life and wants to explore his world. He is cautioned by his mentor, Dumbledore, that 'curiosity is not a sin, but we should exercise caution with our curiosity'. At one point Harry accidentally finds himself in Knockturn Alley (another word play – nocturnally, of the night), a street where dubious people trade in Dark magic and forbidden things. What are the limits of our exploration? Do we have to try everything just because it's there? How far should we delve into the mysteries of science? Should we try taking drugs just to find out what it is like? This is an age that encourages experimentation, especially in the sexual realm, and it does so at an ever younger age. When are we ready for such experiences? The pressure upon many children is extreme and we must discuss with them where to set the limits.

There are many *Harry Potter* websites. Most of these will be at the fun level but hyperlinks will point children to where they can learn 'real' magic. Web filters can be used to block explicit sex, violence and bad language, but not witchcraft. We need to caution our children about exploring these other sites.

Since these books are about witchcraft they raise the question, how shall we view witchcraft in today's world? We are told in *Harry Potter* that the school, Hogwarts, was built 'far from prying Muggle eyes, for it was an age when magic was feared by common people, and witches and wizards suffered much persecution'. The author is giving an opinion here that reflects on real history. It suggests that we should no longer fear witches and wizards since this is a more enlightened age. It's worth discussing why, and indeed to what extent, society persecuted witches in the past, and why they had such fears. While we would not wish to condone killing witches, is there no longer anything to fear? To what extent is it dangerous to engage in witchcraft? What are the possible consequences? Much of the *Harry Potter* witchcraft is far-fetched and quite humorous, but there is a definite serious side and the children at Hogwarts are being trained in its use. Moreover, some of those being trained are already known to be attracted to the Dark side. What does that teach us about the dangers of dabbling in the occult?

At the conclusion of the tale, in his death and 'resurrection', Harry Potter is a partial metaphor for Jesus. In an age when children are taught that all religions are legitimate ways to God, and that there is little difference between the holy man, the Dalai Lama, a shaman, a guru, Buddha, Muhammad and Jesus, we will want to stress the uniqueness of Jesus. He isn't simply the best player on the field; he is quite unique. Others might aspire to be called son of God by virtue of their spiritual achievements. Jesus was for ever the eternal Son of God who laid aside his glory and came for a while to live among us: 'Who, being in very nature God, did not consider equality with God something to be grasped, but made himself nothing, taking the very nature of a servant' (Philippians 2:6–7). The others try to climb up above the mass, whereas Jesus voluntarily came down to join us. The difference raises the question as to whether we save ourselves by our own works of self-improvement or whether we are saved by faith in Christ.

Jesus did his works by the power of the Holy Spirit, and he calls each one of us to do the same. The shaman connects with a spirit by means of channelling and often goes into a trance in order to heal. The Christian seeks for the anointing of the Holy Spirit to flow – a quite different source! Our children can easily feel powerless in today's world, yet they have power available to them in Christ. The spiritual gifts of insight and healing are not just for Christian meetings; they are for the real world of home, school, college and workplace and sports club. We must encourage and train our children in their use. The power available to the Christian is released not through a desire to control but through submission to the will of the Father. So, Jesus did not come to please himself, but to do the will of his Father who sent him.

Luke Skywalker in *Star Wars* abandons his trust in his technical abilities and lets the Force take him over. Harry Potter, in a similar manner, trusts his innate instincts in times of crisis rather than the rules. This raises the question of to what extent we should trust our innate feelings. Have we relied too much on reason? What does it mean to let the Holy Spirit work through us? Many Christians are afraid of feelings and intuition because they have so little experience of the Holy Spirit in their lives. Instead, they live by an unbiblical rationalist world-view that really cuts no ice in a post-modern world. How much can we trust our instincts and do they need tempering with reason? What is the place of visions and symbols in the process of guidance? How can our inexperienced youngsters get it right? Harry Potter's instincts sometimes lead him to break the school rules and the moral ones. We may wish to discuss the place of moral absolutes. What about telling white lies, for example, or stealing to help the poor? Is it justified to bomb innocent people because they are ruled by a dictator that we don't like? When we use the same weapons as evil for good purposes, as Harry is tempted to, what does this tell us about means and ends? Important questions!

Harry Potter is cast as an alienated, autonomous figure, a misfit hero with a special destiny that he sometimes resents. How does this make a Christian child feel in the playground when he is cast as the odd one among unbelievers? Does this help him understand how other minorities feel?

Since spell-casting plays such an important role in the *Harry Potter* books, we should encourage our children in the use of their own spiritual weapons. These are based upon the resounding defeat of Satan at Calvary where Jesus, 'having disarmed the powers and authorities . . . made a public spectacle of them, triumphing over them by the cross' (Colossians 2:15). This is the great spell that dispels all other spells! Thus, the warfare that we engage in is a mopping-up operation; the victory is already assured.

The Christian armour, as described in Ephesians 6:13–18, is all based upon this critical event. Regarding our two attacking weapons, the word of God and prayer, 'though we live in the world, we do not wage war as the world does. The weapons we fight with are not the weapons of the world. On the contrary, they have divine power to demolish strongholds. We demolish arguments and every pretension that sets itself up against the knowledge of God' (2 Corinthians 10:3–5). This being so, we must empower and equip our children in the spiritual use of these weapons.

We should also remind them of the importance of words. Spell-casting in *Harry Potter* is another kind of physics, what we might call psychophysics. Like the martial arts, it operates by intention, technique and belief, i.e. willpower, all concentrated into the blow – or the words of the spell. This might in fact be drawing on unmentioned occult sources – that is, the practitioner may believe it is his will that is producing the effect when in actuality it is a demonic force. This is something we need to discuss with our children.

However, there is a further point. The oft-quoted taunt, 'Sticks and stones may break my bones, but your words can never hurt me', is anything but true. Words can be incredibly destructive. In *Harry Potter* this point is made regarding the illegal 'killing curse'. To use it merits a one-way ticket to Azkaban – hell on earth. While this is the punishment for murder in *Harry Potter*, Jesus makes the same point in the Sermon on the Mount concerning murderous words. 'You have heard that it was said to the people long ago, "Do not murder, and anyone who murders will be subject to judgment." But I tell you that anyone who is angry with his brother will be subject to judgment. Again, anyone who says to his brother, "Raca," is answerable to the Sanhedrin. But anyone who says, "You fool!" will be in danger of the fire of hell.' (Matthew 5:21–22).

Words have immense power to curse or to bless. By them we will be justified or condemned, and James reminds us that the tongue is unruly and needs to be tamed (*see* James 3:5–10). It is a lesson we must all learn but one that is especially important in our formative years. Some words should still be taboo when used in anger, and cursing people is always wrong.

What should we do when people use insulting and cursing words against us? We should remind ourselves that

Jesus bore the curse for us on the cross and thereby destroyed its power to harm us. This is our great counter-spell. It is one way of using the sword of the Spirit, which is the word of God. Then, rather than cursing in return, we should bless, thereby disarming our enemies of their real power (*see* Romans 12:17–21).

Remind your children, too, that there are occasions when we are called to speak words of faith in the name of Jesus that bring blessing to others, such as healing. Such words need to come from the heart and after seeking the Lord in prayer. The name of Jesus should not be used superstitiously as a magic formula, yet when it is used responsibly in accordance with God's will we will see the fulfilment of Jesus' words: 'I tell you the truth, if anyone says to this mountain, "Go, throw yourself into the sea," and does not doubt in his heart but believes that what he says will happen, it will be done for him' (Mark 11:23).

Every Christian parent, youth worker and teacher needs to play their part in ensuring that the children in their charge are taught the Christian gospel and the world-view that flows from it. Our children should be trained to share the knowledge of the true and living God for themselves without any need to feel apologetic for their faith. They should be taught how to advise others to shun wrong behaviour and occult activity, without sounding holier-than-thou. We should help them discover their own spiritual gifts and how to use these for the blessing of others. Since Christian children and teenagers are often in a minority, we should encourage them to realise that 'the one who is in you is greater than the one who is in the world' (1 John 4:4). Teach them, too, the value of fellowship with other believers when they are in their secular environment. In fighting this good fight of the faith, our children should be supplied with good scriptures and good prayers that address their common needs and that, under the anointing of the Holy Spirit, really do change the spiritual climate.

We set out to examine some of the most significant trends in our culture and the way that they affect our children. In referring to the *Harry Potter* books I have tried to be even-handed and have left it to those with children to decide whether or not the books are suitable reading matter for their particular charges. This will not please everyone, but the alternative of a prescribed list of reading matter too easily absolves us from our responsibility to think for ourselves. Training up a child in the way he should go is not something we can pass on to others, least of all the secular media. It is our task and we must do it prayerfully and wisely.

Many forces, for good and ill, seek to bend and shape the minds of our children. Whether those minds finish up as beautiful living sculptures or as warped, distorted messes will depend very largely upon the values that are embedded early on in their experience. The gospel of our Lord Jesus Christ, and all works of art, science, literature and entertainment that encourage compassionate realism in our care for others, coupled with noble aspirations to be the people God intended us to be, can all work together to produce a generation that is confident, robust, wise and merciful. May such children fight the good fight of the faith and change the world for the better.

Appendix

Some Harry Potter names and places

The *Harry Potter* series:
    Harry Potter and the Philosopher's Stone
       (in the USA *Harry Potter and the Sorcerer's Stone*)
    Harry Potter and the Chamber of Secrets
    Harry Potter and the Prisoner of Azkaban
    Harry Potter and the Goblet of Fire
    Harry Potter and the Order of the Phoenix
    Harry Potter and the Half-Blood Prince
    Harry Potter and the Deathly Hallows

Harry Potter	– the hero
Ron Weasley	– the pal
Hermione Granger	– the swot
Ginny Weasley	– Ron's younger sister
Hagrid	– a soppy half-giant
Dobby	– a liberated house elf
Malfoy	– school bully
Dumbledore	– headmaster

Severus Snape	– head of Slytherin House
McGonagall	– head of Gryffindor House
Sirius Black	– Harry's godfather
Dementors	– state torturers
Voldemort	– the Dark Lord
Tom Riddle	– Voldemort's real name
Dursleys	– Harry's Muggle guardians
Muggles	– non-wizards
Mudbloods	– wizards with two Muggle parents
Half-bloods	– wizards with one Muggle parent or grandparent
Squibs	– children of wizards but with no magic ability
Cornelius Fudge	– Ministry of Magic boss
Dolores Umbridge	– Ministry official and High Inquisitor of Hogwarts
Hogwarts	– school of witchcraft and wizardry
Hogsmeade	– the only entirely wizarding village in Britain
Diagon Alley	– the secret wizarding shopping street in London
Gringotts	– the wizarding bank run mainly by Goblins
Quidditch	– an aerial sport